Ráfaga

Portrait of Ráfaga, 1988, by Pablo Beteta, Managua. Photograph by J. K. Wilson.

Ráfaga

The Life Story of a Nicaraguan Miskito Comandante

By Reynaldo Reyes and J. K. Wilson

Edited by Tod Sloan

University of Oklahoma Press / Norman and London

To our mothers

Manuela
Sara Jo
Lois

Royalties will be used to support the education of Miskito youths through the Reynaldo Reyes Miskuyo Scholarship Fund.

Library of Congress Cataloging-in-Publication Data

Reyes, Reynaldo, 1943–
    Ráfaga : the life story of a Nicaraguan Miskito Comandante /
Reynaldo Reyes, J.K. Wilson : edited by Tod Sloan.—1st ed.
      p. cm.
    Includes bibliographical references and index.
    ISBN 0-8061-2453-9
    1. Reyes, Reynaldo, 1943–   . 2. Mosquito Indians—Biography.
3. Guerillas—Nicaragua—Biography. 4. Mosquito Indians—Wars.
5. Mosquito Indians—Government relations. 6. Nicaragua—History—
Revolution, 1979—Personal narratives. 7. Nicaragua—Politics and
government—1979–   . I. Wilson, J.K. (Judith Kay), 1943–   .
II. Sloan, Tod Stratton, 1952–   . III. Title.
F1529.M9R497   1992
972.85'00497802—dc20
[B]   92-54141
                                                    CIP

The paper in this book meets the guidelines for permanence and durability of the Committee on Production Guidelines for Book Longevity of the Council on Library Resources, Inc. ∞

Contents

Illustrations

Figures

Map

Preface

by TOD SLOAN

This is the life story of Reynaldo Reyes Davis, a Miskito Indian born on the Atlantic Coast of Nicaragua, who fought with bullets and words for the autonomy and well-being of his people. In these pages we hear how he struggled against poverty to get a basic education; was swept up in the swirl of the Sandinista revolution against a dictator whose greed had impoverished his people; took up arms against the Sandinistas when they committed atrocities against the Miskitos; earned his nom de guerre, "Ráfaga"; gradually became disillusioned by the corruption of the leaders of the "Contra" counterrevolution; and began to work for peace and autonomy through dialogue with the Nicaraguan government. This saga was related first to J. K. Wilson, who painstakingly transcribed and formed into a smooth narrative countless hours of disjointed recountings, questions, retranslations, and retellings. I entered the project in midstream to do further interviewing, check translations, and work over the final version of the narrative with Ráfaga.

Without doubt, this book will be picked up and read by a wide assortment of readers. Some will read it out of pure human interest, wondering, "Who is this Ráfaga fellow?" They will not be disappointed. The juxtaposition of his particular personality with the social and political situation of his Miskito people produced a life trajectory, and now a life story, that will fascinate, educate, and inspire many.

Others will bring their various political agendas to bear on this text. I cannot predict how their views will be affected by

Ráfaga's story. I believe, however, that even extremists will be sobered by this book and will grow in appreciation for the complexity of situations that, from a distance, have been too easy to cast in black and white. They may even see that the views they hold so proudly and comfortably have sometimes been, and continue to be, the cause of unnecessary suffering. In this connection it is necessary to say that J. K. Wilson and I, as well as the numerous people who helped this book come into being and supported us during our work, also had political motives for our involvement. In this vein we must dissociate ourselves from Ráfaga's elation, reported in the Epilogue, in response to Violeta Barrios de Chamorro's 1990 victory over the Sandinistas. That we have nevertheless proceeded with publication serves as evidence that this is indeed Ráfaga's own story, and not an account generated to serve alien political interests.

Still others will come to this book with academic interests, perhaps from the perspective of cultural anthropology, Central American history, or political science. I need to caution these readers that the conditions that gave birth to this text made it nearly impossible to meet all established standards for field-work, translation, documentation, and verification. It would be wrong, for example, to see this as an ethnographic "life history," although some of the content does shed light on cultural processes among contemporary Miskitos. The book falls more clearly into the genre known in psychology as a "life story" or life narrative. It is a man's attempt to tell the story of his life in the way he chooses to tell it. He chose the topics, themes, and issues to address. In some cases he elaborated on these in response to prompting from the listeners. In a few instances he supplied written text, for example, for parts of chapter 11.

In her Preface, J. K. Wilson explains how the manuscript came to be. Her account will help scholars judge the extent to which they may use this narrative as evidence for whatever projects they may have. My hunch is that they will find it quite useful and reliable in terms of content, but, given the nature of the translation and text construction, it is clear that linguistic and stylistic analyses would be inappropriate. Furthermore, as with any autobiographical material, the book presents the "facts" as Ráfaga sees them. The people who participated in the creation of this book do not apologize for this. They have been interested primarily in getting Ráfaga's story out to the world. It should be known that to do this Ráfaga and J. K. Wilson, his "voice" in English, have taken great risks and made endless personal sacrifices. For their efforts on this book, they will receive no financial gain. Royalties due the authors will be placed in a trust fund for scholarships for young Miskitos orphaned by the war in Tawaswalpa (the Miskito term for the Atlantic Coast of Nicaragua; also once called Tulu Walapa).

Finally, it is important to acknowledge the readers whom Ráfaga is most interested in reaching: his own Miskito people, other indigenous groups, and those who are working for the restoration of rights to the indigenous peoples of Nicaragua, of the Americas, and of the world. They will find in his story a stimulating example of the wisdom, courage, and persever-ance that will continue to be necessary through the coming decades if the political autonomy of indigenous nations is to be successfully realized.

Preface

by J. K. WILSON

My primary intention in producing this book is to give the reader a sense of what life is like on the Miskito Coast, that portion of Nicaragua and Honduras that skirts the Caribbean and is commonly called the Atlantic Coast. A particularly vivid means of conveying that sense is by presenting the life story of a remarkable citizen of the Miskito Coast, Reynaldo Reyes Davis—"Ráfaga."

Before I explain how I came to select Ráfaga as the subject of this life story, however, I must first give an account of how life's journey brought me, a forty-three-year-old mother of three adult children, a registered nurse and graduate student, to a war zone sixty miles south of the Río Coco on Nicaragua's Atlantic Coast.

On the morning after Ronald Reagan's reelection in 1984, I ceased being a silent observer and turned all of my energies toward direct action against what I believed was an immoral intervention by my country in the lives of the people of Nicaragua. At that time I happened to be pursuing graduate studies in cultural anthropology at the University of Tulsa. Trying to find a connection between my prior experience with Caribbean cultures, my interest in Nicaragua, and my academic work, I soon found that little was known in North America about contemporary life on the Miskito Coast. This piqued my curiosity. Simultaneously, through course work and reading, I became convinced of the utility of life history methods in anthropological research.

Early in 1985 I began trying to secure a position in nursing on Nicaragua's Atlantic Coast. I hoped that this work would provide a context for life historical research while also helping people in the region. There was no one in Oklahoma to teach me the Miskito language, but I knew that the Creoles there, descendants of African slaves brought by the British, spoke English, so I pursued only light studies in Spanish. For two long and frustrating years I corresponded with various officials at the Nicaraguan embassy in Washington, exploring ways I might gain entrance into the country to work as a nurse. All attempts were unsuccessful. In January 1987 I applied for work through the Central American Health Rights Network, a U.S.-based organization that provides medical supplies and personnel for humanitarian projects in Nicaragua. Within one week after making application, I was contacted by the coordinators of a construction brigade that was scheduled to go in March to build a "house of peace," the Casa de la Paz, in Puerto Cabezas, a multiethnic community affectionately called Port. The house was to provide temporary residence for individuals coming to the Atlantic Coast to help in rebuilding of communities destroyed by the war and to help with farming, medical, and educational projects in and around Puerto Cabezas. My role in the brigade was that of medical *responsable*.

Travel to Nicaragua's Atlantic Coast is heavily restricted. Whereas technical visas for up to a year are issued for other parts of the country, several varieties of government permission and special limited visas are required in order to spend even one day on the Atlantic Coast. In the case of the construction brigade, government permission to stay for one month had been secured by the coordinators after months of negotiation and planning. This was not much time for building a house or for documenting a life story. But it was a little piece of time, and that was a great deal more than I had been able to obtain through my countless requests to the Nicaraguan embassy.

The travel restrictions turn out to be completely justified. On the Miskito Coast there is little food, insufficient housing, and minimal transportation. No telephone lines connect the Atlantic and Pacific regions. Nonresidents are thus a troublesome burden. The seventeen members of the brigade brought beans, rice, powdered milk, and dried foods so we would not add to the food shortage. We lived in one house together and traveled on foot.

WORKING IN PORT

Many obstacles prevented the brigade from keeping to the original schedule once we were in Port. The site, which was donated by the government, had not been cleared of its existing structure. Also, certain tools, equipment, and building materials that the brigade had sent by boat through Canada (to bypass the U.S. trade embargo) to Puerto Cabezas had been stored in a variety of places. Those items had to be found and brought to the site. Slowly, the task of bringing down and digging up twenty-eight concrete footings, which had fastened the previous structure securely to the ground, was underway.

Our work began each morning at about six o'clock. We stopped at noon because of the intense heat, hotter than the hottest Oklahoma summer I had ever experienced. Siesta was from noon to three P.M., after which work would resume, continuing until about six each evening.

During the siesta hours some of us would visit churches, schools, and families in the community. I took advantage of this time to begin looking for a subject who could speak English and who would allow me to conduct a series of interviews. While visiting the hospital, I met a strong-spirited nurse named Edna who functioned as the facility's administrator. She declined my life story proposal, saying that her life was "insignificant," which, in my opinion, it was not. I accepted her unwillingness to cooperate with the project, and I continued with the task of looking for a subject.

In the evenings various community groups would come to *casa* no. 18, where the brigade members were housed, to discuss with us the circumstances of their lives, their communities, and the ways in which their organizations were attempting to help the people, preserve culture, and strengthen the institutions so that all would survive the effects of the war.

One of the first groups that came to talk with our brigade at *casa* no. 18 was KISAN por la Paz, a group of repatriated Miskito warriors in favor of peaceful dialogue with the Sandinistas. Their spokesman and leader, Reynaldo Reyes, was accompanied by bodyguards with pistols tucked in their pants. He spoke to us through his translator, Helen Duffy, an American woman residing in Port since marrying a Nicaraguan.

At that first meeting with KISAN por la Paz, Sandinista representatives were present in what appeared to be observer roles. Those Sandinistas did not speak during the dialogue between our brigade and Reynaldo, but they were listening to every word said. It was evident that this Miskito leader had a keen grasp of the circumstances enveloping his people, along with a courageous and intelligent program of how the Indians could best preserve their lives and their culture while at the same time building a respectful friendship with the government, which many had militarily opposed in the recent past. All of this information was related to us in a smooth, articulate way, enhanced throughout by the leader's charisma.

All those present, including the government representatives, had their attention fastened tightly to the man who was speaking. A certain depth beneath his expression and his words reminded me of Robert Kennedy in the way he was able to connect with the people present, inspire them, and energize them toward participation in the vision he was outlining.

At the time, the idea never arose in my mind to consider him as the subject for this project. He was atypical, he did not speak English, and I had no way of gaining access to this powerful leader. In the days and weeks that followed, our group was visited by many leaders of various groups, but none was as dynamic as Reynaldo Reyes. During those days remaining, the Miskito leader would interject himself from time to time into our building project by working side by side with us. Always his bodyguards were close by, and always he spoke to us through a translator. He said, "This is how we build a strong peace. We work together, sweat together, and learn together."

While the brigade's construction process was proceeding, I continued to look for a subject to interview in the free time available to me. I had no systematic method for making this critical choice and was depending on intuition and circumstance. At the conclusion of a Creole Cultural Club meeting, which was attended by a group of our *brigadistas*, I met a black woman named Carolyn Bush who was outspoken in the English language and who demonstrated a friendliness and a risk-taking spirit that encouraged me to make the proposal to her. She accepted the idea with a comfortable willingness, and we began the interviews the next day.

Tape recorder, pencil, and paper in hand, I walked from our construction site to Carolyn's house every day at siesta time. There for about three to four hours each day we engaged in an interview process. Carolyn is a baker, a mother, and a grandmother whose daily life is full of activity in those roles as well as the role of neighborhood leader. It was a joy to work each day with her, and it was easy to become friends. It became evident to me about one week before the expiration of our visas that the three or four hours spent each day with her were not going to allow a sufficient amount of time for the completion of the interviews. At this point, I apologetically reduced my participation in the construction project so that I could have more hours in the remaining days to collect the data for the life story.

During the last week in Port, Carolyn and I did everything together from morning until night. We baked bread, attended neighborhood meetings, and went to church, all the while with the tape recorder running. Walking from one place to another, we used every minute recording the events of her life through a question-and-answer process. Many meaningful events had helped to create this delightful middle-aged Creole woman, who was not only the subject of a life story but also, by this time, my friend.

In that final week there was a Contra attack on a government truck transporting recently repatriated Miskito families from Puerto Cabezas up to their villages on the Río Coco. Forty-two Indian children were kidnapped by the attackers, causing the whole community to be filled with feelings ranging from concern to outrage. The churches organized an ecumenical six-hour prayer vigil in behalf of the missing children, which I attended along with hundreds of men, women, and children from all ethnic and religious groups.

The following episode in my account would typically be omitted out of respect for anthropology's realist and antimystical values, but the experience was crucial in changing the direction of my thought and is therefore included. While I was participating in that prayerful group expression, sitting on a wooden bench in the next-to-last row, I suddenly felt "lifted up" from my seat in a spiritual sense by a powerful presence, which I recognized as one having visited me only once before in my lifetime some twenty years earlier. Instantly I tried to make sense of it, but could not grasp the meaning. I looked to the front and to the sides, but all I could see and hear seemed only to confirm the event of the vigil. Confounded by that intangible celestial jabbing, I turned to look directly behind me. Sitting there was Reynaldo Reyes, who apparently had come into the vigil after me. His eyes were fixed on the congregation. I sensed a numinous force. After seeing him and relating my eccentric feeling in some way to his presence at the vigil, I perceived what the old Negro spiritual "God Is Trying to Tell You Something" claims.

For several days after the vigil I did not see the Miskito leader in Port. I heard that an Indian village located in one of the peace zones was under threat of attack and that the Sandinista military had transported him to that community to assume direct command of its defense.

Two nights before our departure, our brigade hosted a party, complete with Heineken beer (a rare treat on the Coast) purchased earlier at the diplomatic store in Managua, the purpose of which was to show our appreciation to all of those people in the community who had shared their time and lives with us. The night of the party was the same night on which Carolyn's granddaughter was to be christened at the Moravian church. I opted for the christening and had left *casa* no. 18 well before the guests had begun to arrive.

As Carolyn and I walked in the dusty street through the black of night after the service, we started to say our good-byes with a promise to write to each other in the months ahead. She told me that the brigade coordinators had invited her to the party, and it was there in the street that the two of us decided to go to the fiesta. As we walked along together, I asked her, for the first time, if she knew Reynaldo Reyes and if she had some opinion about his mission. Her response was vague and uncertain as to who Reyes was, which I thought strange because he was obviously, from what I had observed, a community leader. I told Carolyn that this man had impressed me to such an extent that I felt I should try to speak to him should he be at the party. I was thinking that I wanted to share my personal gratitude with him for his contribution to our education while in Port.

A block away from *casa* no. 18 Carolyn and I could hear the music and the cheerful voices wafting through the tamarind-scented air. As we came upon the group gathered beneath the house, I looked to the far side of the activity, where Reynaldo Reyes was seated in a quiet, erect posture. Not far from him was his translator, Helen Duffy, who was visiting with a group of our *brigadistas*. I grabbed Carolyn's hand and literally dragged her through the music, the conversations, and the dancers to the place where Helen was standing. I said, "Helen, please go with me so that you can translate my words for Reynaldo. I want to speak to him." After I had told her what kind of a message I had for him, she said, "You can tell him that without a translator. He understands a little English."

In an instant I realized that I could have been talking directly to this man whose contributions to his people and to our brigade had been so evident. As Carolyn and I approached him, I started to arrange my thoughts about how I would introduce myself and my friend. But no introduction was needed: when Carolyn saw that it was the Miskito seated in the quietly regal posture whom we were approaching, she opened her arms to embrace him, exclaiming, "Ráfaga! Ráfaga! So you are the one Judy has been trying to tell me about."

Stammeringly I introduced myself, then for what seemed to be an uncomfortably long period of time I tried to convey in English and what little Spanish I knew just how I had been feeling about the importance of his work and about my own hope for the future of his people. I felt awkward about the way my words came out. I kept asking, "Do you understand what I am trying to say?" He would respond, in English, "I understand some little." Regardless of how uncomfortable I felt making this attempt at communication, he was obviously receiving it all with a smile of acceptance.

The next morning, early, Reynaldo Reyes—Comandante "Ráfaga"—came to *casa* no. 18 accompanied by his young son, Lester, to invite me to go with them to the pier "to teach you how to fish Miskito way." Honored by the invitation, I eagerly accepted, then bolted up the stairs to change into clothes more appropriate for the occasion.

On the way to the pier we stopped at a small house, where I was introduced to Reynaldo's mother, Manuela, then we three were joined by two boys smaller than Lester, who were identified as cousins and who carried two large, bulging cloth sacks.

Out on the end of the long wooden pier, which extended perhaps one hundred yards from the shore, Lester began to show me how to catch the bait and put it on the handcrafted hooks. Reynaldo sat some distance away, taking mangos and coconuts from the sacks and preparing them for us while at the same time giving advice in Miskito and Spanish, alternately, to the three boys. There I was, the day before I was to leave Port, at the end of a military target, dragging bare hooks through the water trying to snag live bait while the Miskito chief prepared fruit for me. Mango juice dripping from our chins, we laughed and fished in the sun, most of the time not having a clue of what each was trying to communicate to the other by means of the three languages being spoken. There were no bodyguards present and no talk or evidence of war except for the pockmarks in the pier left by Contra mortars. We were just five people on a pier fishing and eating fruit together. It was an especially joyful time for me.

Thirty minutes later, a Sandinista four-wheel-drive military vehicle suddenly came racing down the pier toward us. It stopped about ten feet from Reynaldo, who had already started walking briskly toward it.

Without a word spoken to Lester by his father, the young

boy began retrieving the fishing lines. A quick conversation between Reynaldo and soldiers, spoken in urgent tones, resulted in the Miskito leader saying to me in English, "I must go. Trouble in Yulo. Come."

The Sandinista soldiers revised their seating positions in the vehicle, then Reynaldo assisted me into the back seat and placed Lester on my lap. As he sat down beside us, the vehicle made a U-turn at the end of the pier, then accelerated as it headed back to shore. I understood Reynaldo to say to the driver, in Spanish, "Take her to house no. 18." Speeding through the streets of Port, we traveled with not another word spoken. I was holding Lester so tightly that I felt bonded to him. A screeching halt and we were in front of *casa* no. 18, where Reynaldo pried Lester from my arms, then climbed out and assisted me to the ground.

I must have been wearing a curious expression because he said to me, "Your face. Your face." Then, placing his hands on my shoulders, he turned my whole body toward him and said, "We have work to make together. We will work together." With those words, he jumped into the military car as it started to move, leaving me standing alone in the middle of the street with the red dirt of Port swirling around me in a vortex of energy which was, in that moment, drawing into its center all that surrounded it. Thus, in a circumstance of synchronicity and because of the souls of two unlikely candidates, a zygote of an idea was conceived. It was not recognizable by form, nor was it clear to either of us, but it was most assuredly present and constituted by a strength inside of ourselves which allowed it to grow and develop.

THE IDEA TAKES FORM

The following day our brigade left Port and returned to Managua, where I began to compose a letter to Reynaldo suggesting we try to communicate in the months ahead in order to define how we might "work together." Describing my plan to write about Carolyn's life, I raised the possibility of combining, in one book, his own story with that of Carolyn's. Also in that initial letter I attempted to explain what an anthropological life history was and how such a project was related to academia. I urged him to take the letter to Helen Duffy or to Carolyn Bush so that it could be translated into Spanish and therefore received by him with as clear an understanding as possible.

During the next seven months a continuous line of letter writing organized itself between Reynaldo, Carolyn, and me. Carolyn became the lifeline, the way through which Reynaldo and I communicated. I would send my ideas in English to Carolyn. She would relate them to Reynaldo in Spanish, then relay to me in English his responses. That campaign culminated in a conference telephone call between myself in Oklahoma, Reynaldo in Managua, and Helen Cohen, a brigade member who translated for us, in San Francisco. The outcome of that conversation was an agreement to meet in Managua during November 1987 to work together. I advised Reynaldo to come fully prepared with information related to dates, places, and eyewitnesses of the events of his life. He would be responsible for securing a translator; I assumed all of the other responsibilities, such as the finances and logistics. We chose Managua because that city was accessible to both of us and because its distance from the Atlantic Coast would allow the process to proceed without interference from the Miskito leader's military responsibilities.

I flew to Managua in November and was met at the airport by Reynaldo, accompanied by all five of his children, three grandchildren, one uncle, and an assortment of bodyguards. We began our work the following day. He informed me that his uncle Abraham would translate for us, because much of the information he wanted to give me was too politically and militarily sensitive to be entrusted to a professional translator, though many were available in Managua.

The first surprise presented itself on our initial day of work. With Uncle Abraham, Reynaldo, and myself present, the tape recorder was turned on. Immediately I sensed Reynaldo's uneasiness. He turned the recorder off, then explained to me through the translator, whose broken English was difficult to understand, that on the advice of the Miskito "old heads" (the council of tribal elders), he would under no circumstances give the data to me unless I would guarantee him that his life history would not in any form be combined with that of the Creole woman, Carolyn Bush.

I was unsettled by this turn of events. Nothing in his letters or phone calls had indicated to me that he was considering such an ultimatum. He demanded that I make a decision on this matter before we began the interviews. I told him that I would have to consider it. The three of us went to a restaurant for coffee, where we discussed the issue for some three hours. In the final event, I chose to give him that guarantee, believing that I was in a remarkably timely position, confronted by an opportunity I could not allow to pass. I knew that the material about Carolyn's life could be organized into a separate piece of work later, and even though I still had good reason to believe that the two histories could exist side by side in one volume, giving the reader a richer description of life on the Atlantic Coast from two ethnic perspectives, I surrendered my guarantee under the conditions specified.

It was during our argument about whether or not Carolyn's life story would be a part of the book that I began to understand Ráfaga's motivation and purpose for wanting his life story and the story of his people published. Ráfaga feared that the few schools that were provided for Miskito children by the Sandinista government were portraying Miskito history in terms favorable to the revolutionary regime. They were obviously incapable of presenting large portions of Miskito history, owing to the old heads' former unwillingness to share their heritage with outsiders. Ráfaga and the old heads had determined that my proposal might very well be their first and final opportunity to have their story recorded. Furthermore, to their knowledge, no Miskito had ever had the opportunity to publish this history or an account of events related to the Sandinista revolution from a Miskito point of view. A variety of histories of the Miskitos had been published, but always as interpreted by people outside the tribe.

The recorder was turned on and the information flowed in a chronological fashion. Time and again we all struggled to clarify and to reach an understanding of what Reynaldo was trying to convey. Those times during the interviews when the most uncomfortable feelings arose were, in reality, evidence of the strength of our commitment to continue and complete the interviews.

Reynaldo understood enough English to sense when the translation from Miskito to English was grossly incorrect. At those times he and Abraham would work through the clarifications in Miskito and in Spanish, then finally the "approved" version would be translated for me into English. Often I was not able to understand an incident's relation to previously described events, in which cases my questions had to pass through the translator to Reynaldo.

The interview process engaged us for three weeks, with the three of us working from about nine each morning until about six each evening. A new location was used each of the three weeks. During the first week we worked at the Hotel Ticomo, a few miles outside Managua. For the second week, Reynaldo chose to work at his family's house. We completed the third week's interviews at Uncle Abraham's Managua residence. Reynaldo's bodyguards were never far away, and security considerations influenced the changing of the work locations. We finished the interviews late one night, then I flew back to Oklahoma the following morning with ninety hours of recorded material and several legal pads filled with handwritten notes.

WRITING THE LIFE STORY

The first phase of my work, that of transcribing the tapes, was tedious and time consuming. It became necessary to establish a new place of residence and postpone graduate studies to devote all of my time, other than my hospital work, to the life story project.

Feeling ashamed to ask Carolyn for her continued go-between services, I began to write directly to Reynaldo. The necessity for him to translate my English and I his Spanish forced us to become better acquainted with each other's language, eventually to the point that we were able to work without the help of a translator. The turnaround time for letters between

Oklahoma and Port being about eight weeks, progress was slow, though ongoing.

The task of writing the life story in a readable narrative began in the early months of 1988. As Reynaldo sent letters and additional tapes from Port, I began to realize that many events had been forgotten or not fully described in the November 1987 interviews. What I had judged to be the end of the work turned out to be, in fact, just the beginning of a new, more complex, stage. It became apparent to both of us that we would have to meet again in order to complete the text. By this time the project had acquired a life of its own, which seemed to compel both of us to do whatever was necessary to allow it to be finished.

Reynaldo applied for U.S. visas for himself and his two youngest children through the American embassy in Managua. That process, like most things one tries to accomplish in Managua, was slow. The visas still had not been granted when I returned to Nicaragua in April 1988. Together, Reynaldo and I visited the embassy to plead a case for visas, but the consulate would issue only one, for Reynaldo. He and I flew to Oklahoma in May 1988, leaving the two young children with their older sisters in Managua, because their invalid mother was unable to care for them.

After his arrival in the United States, our network of "friends of Nicaragua" began asking him to speak to various university and church groups, most of which were located far from Oklahoma. Not wanting to pass up these opportunities to address concerned people about the plight of Indians in Nicaragua, Reynaldo accepted many of those invitations, limiting our time together and hindering the completion of the writing. I became his stenographer, scheduling secretary, travel agent, chauffeur, and translator. Every day there were letters to be answered and proposals to be considered. To complicate the situation further, both of us worried about the two young children left behind in Nicaragua.

In June 1988 Reynaldo accepted an invitation from Indigenous World to accompany some of its members back to Managua, where a U.S. Veterans for Peace convoy was expected. Because the official dedication of the now completed Casa de la Paz was to be celebrated in Port during that time as well, he judged this to be a good opportunity to return to his country to participate in those two events and try once more to bring the small children out.

In July I was notified by telephone from Managua that Reynaldo and the two children were ready to make the trip. I drove to Laredo, Texas, where I met not only Reynaldo and the two children but also (to my surprise) his half brother, along with five squawking, yellow-naped baby parrots, which Reynaldo hoped he could sell in the States to raise some money for Miskito orphans. On July 18, 1988, this assemblage motored across Texas to Oklahoma, where a myriad of new experiences, difficult adjustments, and sweet struggle awaited all.

It took another eleven months to finish the writing. Opportunities to work together on the project were few. Relieved of the concern for the children and progressively becoming more and more fluent in each other's language, Reynaldo and I gave the project our best efforts whenever my hospital schedule and his speaking tour schedule allowed us the time. Professor Tod Sloan, a University of Tulsa psychologist specializing in Third World development and life history methods, joined the project during this phase. Because of his fluency in Spanish, he and Reynaldo were able to amplify rapidly various sections of the manuscript through additional interviews.

The depressed economy in Oklahoma was not a fertile environment to find buyers for the parrots at the prices we had hoped, so we kept holding on to them in hopes that the economy would improve. In the final days of writing, we exiled the birds to the garage, where their trilingual squawking was less bothersome.

Now the writing is finished. The house is quiet. It has been two and one-half years since I stood alone in that vortex of swirling red dirt. Though the wind has long since died down, the energy of that moment continues to radiate outward. The little zygote of an idea conceived in that encounter has reached parturition in the form of the book now in your hands.

Before you leap into the first chapter and become caught up in the grand emotional vista of his initial declarations, please consider that Ráfaga was not the "only good thing to survive the suffering" of his people as described in chapter 1. My own experience has shown me that there are many intelligent and innovative people working for the peace, many having begun long before Ráfaga's decision to enter the Miskito-Sandinista dialogue for peace and autonomy on the Atlantic Coast. In the absence of the husbands and fathers who left their families for war, thousands of Indian, mestiza, and Creole women made and continue to make a remarkable contribution to the political and economic life of the region while simultaneously caring for the needs of their children. As a result of this experience, they have emerged as the leaders of the Atlantic Coast government—for example, Myrna Cunningham, the appointed governor of Northern Zelaya, and Hazel Law, the elected leader of the Autonomy movement. The Sandinista government, from 1984 until its electoral defeat in 1990, encouraged peace and autonomy, although that effort was not reflected in many television reports, books, or newspapers.

Ráfaga chose to make sacrifices at critical points in his life. As a boy of thirteen years, he left his mother to educate himself. As a young husband and father, he sacrificed so that he could help young Miskito boys acquire educational tools needed to support preservation of the Miskito nation. As a mature man, confronted by war and the reasons for war, he sacrificed his soul. As an even older man, faced with the task of writing his life story, which eventually required that he leave his country, he sacrificed his social milieu, his military position, and his political ambitions within his own society. From his experiences and my own I have learned that in order to bring about renewal and improvement of life, people who care about humanity must be willing to sacrifice the most sacred aspects of themselves within those fiery circumstances of opportunity which life provides.

The gravity of the personal risks Ráfaga was taking in publishing his life story was evidenced even during the first few minutes of our interview. In that initial part of his story he spoke passionately about his hatred for the Sandinista government. Much further into the interview process, he related similarly vitriolic accounts of Contra crimes. By confessing his knowledge and feelings about events on both sides of the war, he has put his life on the line. No matter where he decides to live or travel during the rest of his life, he can expect revenge from parties on either side of the conflict.

The reader may wish to ponder with me these questions: How does a man who has demonstrated anger and violence toward a government finally come to the peace table? How does a man test the religious principles he has been taught and come to new understandings of that faith in relation to nature?

One might consider relationships between the superpowers and the indigenous peoples of the world. Will the insecurity of the superpowers ever allow for the autonomy and cultural integrity of the indigenous world? Will a knowledge of how the U.S. Central Intelligence Agency dealt with the Miskito Indians cause readers to oppose future situations where tribal people are recruited to do the "dirty work" for the world's most powerful nations?

This is the narrative of a contemporary Miskito Indian in Nicaragua who has testified with special authorization from the tribal council of old heads. In the interest of readability I have included neither my prompting questions nor my reactions. I have added a few footnotes and bracketed phrases to amplify or clarify the narrative. Ráfaga's account first describes his youth and how he participated with the Sandinistas in overthrowing the Somoza regime in 1979. It then explains how he and his people were persuaded by Miskitos with ties to the CIA to "overthrow" the Sandinista government. Ráfaga emerged as a commander of Miskito counterrevolutionaries and director of intelligence. In view of his people's suffering in a unwinnable war, Ráfaga finally collaborated with the Sandinistas in an innovative and distinctively democratic process to bring peace and autonomy to the Miskito homeland. This life story provides a window onto the tribe's present and past culture, its power brokers, and the savage disruptions the war has visited upon it. Ráfaga's narrative argues, "from the native's point of view," for the preservation of the cultural integrity and autonomy of tribal peoples.

ACKNOWLEDGMENTS

Many people have provided constructive criticism and support through the past several years of work. I wish to express my gratitude to the Peace Ship/Peace House Construction Brigade and to the Sandinista government of Nicaragua for inviting me to that country and treating me as an honored guest. Special "friends of Nicaragua" who continually gave me moral support are Helen Cohen, Roger Clapp, and Roxanne Dunbar Ortiz.

In Oklahoma, friends and family lovingly and generously gave their time and support. Special thanks to Reverend Jerry Capps and his wife, Alberta, along with the entire B Street Church of God congregation; also to the principal, counselors, and teachers of Cherokee Elementary School. Pat Moss, a Cherokee medicine man, and Adrien Ruby, D.V.M., extended their North American Indian hands in friendship, which always uplifted our spirits. L. G. Graham helped me to synthesize my feelings and thoughts at the conclusion of the writing. Two very special persons, Shirley Leathers and Jeanne Sherrill, gave me the emotional support that made the struggle so dear. Leonard Zusne, Lamont Lindstrom, and Tod Sloan, all at the University of Tulsa, gave me encouragement and instruction, which left me with the confidence to initiate and complete this work.

For her guidance and eternal love of Nicaragua, Maya Miller deserves more praise than words can express. She is a beacon of light to those of us who love the Third World and despise war.

I would like to give special acknowledgment to photographer Lee Shapiro, whose vision of a better world was grounded in his empathy for the plight of this world's less fortunate. Lee will be remembered for his great courage and determination. Also,

1. Awastara
2. Lake Awastara
3. Bonanza
4. Puerto Cabezas (Bilwi)
5. Sandy Bay (Ninayari)
6. Managua
7. Chontales
8. Zone of New Guinea
9. Bluefields
10. Waspam
11. Bihmuna
12. Tronquera
13. Cabo Gracias a Dios (Sita Awala—Old Cape)
14. Bom (Boon)
15. Kum
16. Bilwaskarma
17. Leimus
18. San Alberto
19. San Carlos
20. Puerto Isabel
21. Prinzawala
22. Tipitapa
23. Wawabar
24. Lamlaya
25. Dakura
26. Pahara
27. Miskito Keys
28. Twibila
29. RusRus
30. Sumobila
31. Bihmuna Lagoon
32. Kaulkira (Cauquira)
33. Centro de Instrucción Militar (CIM)
34. Puerto Lempira
35. Puesto de Comando
36. Miskut
37. Lakiatara
38. Yulo
39. Sannilaya
40. Seven Benk
41. Krukira
42. Tuara
43. Iralaya
44. Muku Hill
45. Esperanza
46. Francia Sirpe
47. Karawala
48. Siuna
49. Cola Blanca Mt.
50. Wisconsin
51. Zone Franca
52. Mocoron
53. Saupuka
54. Base no. 50
55. Sisin
56. Saklin
57. Wasla
58. Santa Marta
59. Auyapihni
60. Bom-Sirpe
61. Lidakura
62. Awasyari
63. Kahtkah
64. Rahwa-Unta
65. Kistawan
66. Tuapi
67. Sukatpin
68. Lapan
69. Dakban
70. Ulan Awala
71. Kambla
72. Tegucigalpa

Note: Zona Especial 1 = Northern Zelaya; Zona Especial 2 = Southern Zelaya

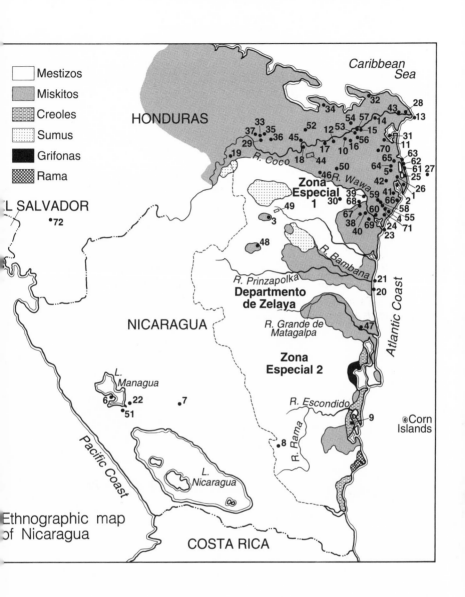

Ethnographic map of Nicaragua

thanks are extended to his widow, Mrs. Linda Shapiro, for her kind permission to use Lee's photographs. Lee Shapiro was murdered during a freelance filming trip in Afghanistan, October 9, 1987.

We are especially grateful to Derrill Bazzy, who during a trip to the Atlantic Coast in September 1989 went out of his way to deliver to Ráfaga's mother an audiotape from her son, who was not able to be with her during her last days. Manuela Chavarria Bilis died of cancer in Awastara on October 18, 1989. Derrill Bazzy's photograph of Manuela on her deathbed was the last representation seen by Ráfaga of his mother's face.

Finally, to my children—Steven, Remy, and Stanley, Jr.— thank you for standing by me. Most important, to my parents, Kay and Sara Jo Wilson, I thank you for all of the endless hours of proofreading, your constant love, your strength, and your faith in me and this project.

Ráfaga

One / Kumi

No One to Protect Us

In the Indian villages on the Atlantic Coast of Nicaragua, we have our own way of living. We like to live in freedom. The people of Awastara, the village where I was born, like to live and think independently. Since the ancient days, we Miskito Indians have possessed great strength and wisdom, which have served to preserve and protect our traditions, our lives, and our dignity as a nation. In our Miskito villages, we exist as brothers and sisters who share one great spirit father. Our spiritual family embraces all Indians who have tread upon this earth and all who will make life's journey in a future time.

Historically, we Miskito have received the respect of those who came to live in our territory as good neighbors in the family of man. But now, in my lifetime, we have been robbed of our rights as an indigenous people. We have been disowned by our neighbors, the Nicaraguans, who have prevented us from exercising our right to life and to freedom. All of civilization has forgotten us in the midst of our troubles. There is no one to protect us.

Now, in the year 1987, I, Ráfaga, am demanding the restoration of our Miskito Indian rights. The voices of all my ancestors and the voices of all future generations of Miskito come now to mingle with my own as our words ride together on a gust of wind, a *ráfaga*, exploding a volley of fiery evidence into the ears of the world.

People of the Earth, Listen to the trouble we have been

3

passing through! Hear our proud voices and participate with us in a congenial spirit and on equal terms!

I acknowledge my personal responsibility and my moral obligation to make this reclamation. I am a Miskito Indian who, like other humans, is capable of kindness and compassion, which I demonstrate in my concern for the needs of my brothers and sisters and in my endeavors to alleviate their suffering. I ask that you look upon us as a people and come together with us in a universal civil conscience. I believe that the intelligent people of the world want to come together. I, Ráfaga, want this union to be a reality.

Today, the Miskito people will see one of our own race lift up our nation for all the world to see. I am struggling in my state of human imperfection to be courageous enough and competent enough to facilitate the return of our freedoms. When I hear my people singing songs about this hero Ráfaga and his bold missions carried out in their behalf, I feel a little embarrassed by the grandeur of the lyrics; however, I confess that the loving sentiments expressed in the musical energy inspire me to remain constant in a noble purpose.

The Sandinista government treated us like lower animals. These men put my brothers in jails, which are now full of the broken spirits of once free Indians. They stole from us, taking all that we had. They raped our young women and beat our men and boys. To treat us that way was not right at all. It was wrong, what they did to humans like us. We are not intellectually or morally inferior to the Spanish. I believe they must have forgotten that Miskitos are people, too. Why else would they have done all of these things to my race?

The Miskitos asked the new government for a few simple things. We asked for our human rights. And for that we were persecuted. For many years before the Sandinistas came to power, we were subjected to neglect by the dictatorship of the Somoza family, but that was a blessing compared to the brutal malevolence of the Sandinistas.

I have seen my own people subjected to barbaric maliciousness when we had no one to sustain us or to protect us. I feel sad when I remember these events of my lifetime. It is painful to us to have been forced to exist in that way.

The atrocities undermined our confidence as a people. They disheartened and confused us. In the worst of our troubles, no one could foresee any good thing that would survive the suffering. But out of that suffering has come a Miskito Indian who is trying his best to make the whole world know about us, and that Miskito is I, Ráfaga.

Awastara

Awastara is a Miskito word that means "big pine tree." This community on the Atlantic Coast, fifty miles north of Puerto Cabezas, is one of the best little villages you could ever look upon. Pine trees circle the village, and on one side lies a beautiful, calm lake, Lake Awastara.

On the seventeenth day of December 1943, I was created, Reynaldo Reyes Davis, in Awastara, Nicaragua. I was the first child born to a young Indian woman, Manuela Davis Reyes. My father, Aleman Reyes Kingsman, also Miskito, died nine months after I was born, when he became ill with smallpox. At that time, he was only twenty-one years old.

Since I never knew my father, I have always had a compelling curiosity about him. I am his only child. My mother and my uncle Abraham Pinner, who was a boyhood friend of my father's, tell me that Aleman left Awastara at the age of eighteen to work in the Bonanza gold mine. Uncle Abraham and mother say that my father was a good fellow with a kind heart who never fought, drank liquor, or made jokes about people. Others whom I have questioned also have spoken well of my father's character. I have been told that he was not a tall man, perhaps five feet six inches, with dark skin like mine and pretty hair. Having come from the mines, his teeth were fixed with fine gold, and he was considered quite good looking.

Aleman had only a bit of formal education, but he was respected by the people for his good mind and Christian habits. Mother believes that I favor my father in physical appearance

6

and in my ways of behaving. Old people who knew him tell me that Aleman never made any kind of trouble and that he respected, loved, and cared for the people of Awastara during the few years that God spared his life.

During my father's short illness, he was looked after by his young wife, my mother, and by his parents. Uncle Abraham came to visit at his bedside every day to sing the hymns my father loved, to pray with him, and to read Bible verses over him. Many say they remember that Aleman had a fine singing voice and that he loved to sing all kinds of songs—Moravian hymns, Miskito folk songs, and English love songs as well.

The old people say they loved my father and were greatly saddened by his death at such a young age. Uncle Abraham was not present at the exact moment of Father's passing; however, he arrived a few minutes later after having been awakened at three-thirty in the morning by the tolling church bells, whose message, he knew, was grim. He went immediately with his sister to the house of Aleman and Manuela, where the young life of my father had just ended. There he sat up with my father's remains for the rest of the night. The next morning Father was put into a plain wooden box, which was then borne upon the shoulders of his young Miskito friends, who carried him to the Awastara cemetery. Everyone from Awastara came to the Moravian funeral, and plenty cried.

I have his grave fixed up nicely, with an iron fence around it. Someday I will make a vault over this place and carve my father's name into the stone. I think that I will always long to know my father, since all who knew him tell me that my voice sounds the same as his and that my gait and gestures are those of Aleman.

In the not too distant future, all who knew my father will have themselves passed on, and there will be no one left to answer my questions or to share with me even one more remembrance of that young friend of Awastara. That is why I hurry now to talk to the old people. Not long ago, an old man in Puerto Cabezas said to me, "Ráfaga, you always want to know more about your papa. Know yourself, Ráfaga. You are your father's son."

My mother, who is living still,* is full-blooded Miskito Indian. She speaks no language other than Miskito and until 1980 could neither read nor write. When she was a young girl, there was no written Miskito alphabet. Now we have an alphabet, and a few books, such as the Bible, have been translated into our language. After the [Sandinista] Triumph in 1979, all of the people of Nicaragua participated in a literacy campaign. Those who knew how to read taught those who did not, and my mother learned how to write her name and how to read.

She is a kindhearted woman who had to raise me without the help of a husband. That is the way it had to be, and that is how it was until I was five.

Mother was a member of the Moravian church when she and my father married. She had joined the church at a tender young age after acknowledging that she understood the meaning of and necessity for moral behavior. Mother has been taking communion since that time. We Indians are a religious people, especially when it comes to taking communion. That is, we really believe in the Lord Jesus Christ.

Mother believes that there is hell below and there is God above and glory in heaven. She taught me this when I was a small boy. So, I took communion also when I was very young like my mother before me.

I remember Mother always being helpful and loving with our people. That is her way because she has a true belief in God. I care for her plenty because I know how difficult it was for her to raise me and how hard her life has been.

When I was four, I got sick with typhoid fever. My mother and grandmother carried me forty-six miles to the town of Puerto Cabezas, where I was treated by Dr. Mangalo, who kept me hospitalized for eight long months. Well, that lady, my mother, because she was poor and widowed, paid that entire bill only with the help of the good Lord.

Soon after I recovered from that illness, Mother married again. She and Koban Chavarria Bilis have since raised ten

*Reyes's mother has since died—on October 18, 1989.

children. Including myself, mother has raised and educated eleven children. Here are the names and approximate ages as of 1988 of my half brothers and half sisters, the children of Manuela Davis and Koban Chavarria, who are still living in Puerto Cabezas:

Asila	F	40
Karolina	F	39
Gustavo	M	38
Sidonia	F	37
Nadilia	F	35
Fermin	M	34
Marcelino	M	33
Blandino	M	32
Roger	M	30
Kano	M	29

Out of respect for my mother, I am trying my best to be competent and loving in order to create a better life for our Miskito people. I am trying to show them by my own example how best to live in this world. Not only my mother, but most of the Miskito people manifest what the Bible teaches. I ask my people, "What must be the first principle in life?" And I always remind them that this must be "to love God." My mother did not know how to read or write, yet through her love and belief in God she created a strong and intelligent foundation upon which my brothers and sisters and I have built our lives. Even now, every morning after I awaken I give thanks to God first, then I go to see my mother and kiss her. The whole town knows about this long-standing tradition of mine.

My earliest memory is that of wanting to go to school. I was barely five when the Moravian church began a program of formal education for the children of Awastara. The school required that each beginning student be no less than seven years of age. Well, this excluded me, and I was loud and persistent in the complaints I made to my mother. The harassment increased each day as I watched the older children going to the schoolhouse. Day and night I annoyed Mother with my grievance, until at last the weight of my scandalous behavior had become so great upon her heart that she went to the school to talk to the teacher about allowing me to be admitted without having met the age requirement.

Mother pleaded with Mr. Huffington to admit me to first grade. I suppose he must have realized this was no ordinary request but the desperate appeal of a mother who could not bear another moment of harassment from this five-year-old boy whose ferocious desire to attend school could not be ignored.

Mr. Huffington, a Miskito Indian of the Moravian faith who is still alive today, taught all of the Indian children of Awastara for five glorious years, until he was transferred to a school in another community, in 1953, I believe. So from the ages of five to nine, my life was filled with the excitement of learning.

When I was growing up in Awastara, the Indians were accustomed to beating their children. Now they are leaving that custom. Sometimes I would make a little mistake and one of my mother's brothers would beat me with a strap. That was the custom. Usually, only the uncle had the right to beat a child. I do not feel any resentment toward my uncles. It was just the custom among our people.

I remember that schooling was not of much importance to the older generations because they never had any formal education and could not appreciate our love for it. For me, going to school was the most important part of my life, and the beatings I remember most clearly were the result of my insolent behavior on those occasions when I had objected to some errand or favor requested of me that interfered with my attendance at school.

I remember such an occasion, when one of my uncles asked me to deliver a message to his friend who lived in another community. It took a whole day to walk there and another day to walk back. I missed two days of school. On my return to class, I proudly but gently eased my rump, which still bore the evidence of my uncle's belt, into the chair.

My childhood was similar to that of any Miskito child. Not much has changed for Miskito children since then, either. The poverty of my people is great. Everybody suffers—the parents, the children, the animals. Basic needs are not met. We manage to survive in thousands of different ways. For example, we worked for the transnational mines as well the lumber and fishing companies. We profited little from that work. Those companies exploited our fish and lumber and minerals but left no schools or clinics. Our fathers earned fifteen cents an hour. The women encircled the industries doing business of various sorts, doing laundry, running kitchens. I worked bringing firewood to my aunts' kitchens, where one fed thirty men and the other fifteen. I had to go three or four miles to get a big load of firewood. I made trips to the creek to bring back two five-gallon water cans on my shoulder up a long, steep slope. Hundreds of children worked from the age seven or eight years on. They earned about five cordobas a week. (Seven cordobas equaled one U.S. dollar in the 1950s.) My biggest wish was to buy shoes and underwear, which I finally got when I was nine, but only after first buying my mother a dress.

There was plenty of land for farming, but the soil in my home region is less rich than in the Río Coco area to the north. There yucca, rice, beans, plantain, and other crops grow easily. We were lucky to have fish to supplement our crops, because our fields only produced enough to eat for six months. We bartered salted fish for food from other areas. To get cash to survive, we had to send our young men to fish for sharks, lobster, and tortoises to sell in Puerto Cabezas. We always waited with great expectation for their return in the catboat from Puerto Cabezas, because they often brought food and supplies that we desperately needed.

We lived in palm-roofed houses of about fifteen by twenty feet, with wood floors raised about four feet above the ground to get fresh air and to keep us above the insects. Up to ten people could live in such a house. The houses were used mostly during the night because we worked all day—we Miskitos don't take siestas like the Spaniards. We often walked, rode on horseback, or canoed ten miles or more to get to the spots where we had planted our crops, leaving at two in the morning and returning at four in the afternoon, to sleep again at seven. There were no nighttime diversions besides making

children. No parks, no movies, no playing fields. Children ran
and swam by instinct, played baseball with homemade sticks
and balls of natural rubber that made everybody hit homeruns.
Our gloves were made from rags and leather. We also played
with homemade tops, kites, and marbles. Sometimes we just
ran and ran, ten times around a one- or two-mile circuit through
the bush. Fishing also was a sport for the kids. In certain
months of spring the freshwater swamps were full of catfish
and *mojara*. In the winter we fished in the sea with nets, because
lots of fish came in to get the shrimp then. It was a healthy life
and few of us got fat, since survival required so much exercise.
The sea and the sun itself seem to cure many illnesses and
kept our skin clean and tan.

Despite this pleasant picturé, it was a life of scarcity, depriva-
tion, and hard work. We also suffered from occasional plagues
and parasites. I remember when I was about ten, the *sukia*
(shaman) predicted that a fever would come that he could not
cure. A dozen children died in a short period. There was no
clinic, nor doctor, except in Puerto Cabezas, where there were
indigenous nurses and white Moravian missionary doctors. As
a child I visited them when I had smallpox and once when I fell
from a fruit tree against the side of a house, hitting my chin on
a window. I couldn't eat for a week and had to be fed intrave-
nously. There is still no doctor or hospital at the Miskito village
in Awastara. The Sandinistas built a clinic there, but it is empty.

When I was barely eleven years old, I had my first experience
of love and sex. I had no idea what these things were. If I failed
to relate this part of my story, it would be incomplete, so I am
making an effort to remember this first love from more than
thirty years ago.

Of course, before this experience I was aware of sex. I had
played "mama-and-papa" with a few girls of my age, and in
these childish games, I had kissed and even pretended to have
sex, but none of that was serious.

A while after Mr. Huffington left, the Moravian church sent a
new teacher to my village, a beautiful young woman about
twenty-five years old. She was part Spanish and part Miskito,
fairly tall, cinnamon-skinned, with beautiful long hair, of which

she was very proud. Many young Indians fell madly in love with her.

I was going through fourth grade with her. I already knew how to read and write pretty well. This woman, whose name I will keep to myself, invited me and my cousin Rafael to sleep at the school building where she was living, because she was afraid. I told her that I would, but that I would have to get my mother's permission. She talked to my mother and got my mother's kind permission for me to accompany her. She had always paid a lot of attention to me and often called me over to talk with her during recess, asking me questions about all sorts of things and talking about whatever.

So, Rafael and I spent two nights sleeping on tables that she had set up for us in the schoolroom, and she slept in her bed in a room on the side of the building. The third night, she woke me up around nine (which is quite late in our tropical communities) and asked me to accompany her because she was cold. I went to her bed and fell asleep. Later she woke me up and told me, "Listen. Rafael is snoring, but I don't want you to sleep, I want you to embrace me." I said yes and embraced her. Then she told me to take off my pants, which made me anxious because I didn't have underwear, but I took them off. Then she told me that I was a well-made little man, that my body was a man's body, and that my heat was that of a man. She then asked me if I knew how to kiss well and I said yes, thinking of the kisses I had practiced while playing "mama-and-papa." So she said, "Kiss me." I kissed her and she said, "That's not the way to kiss. Do you want to learn how?" "Yes, yes." I remember that she kissed me all over my body—my feet, the palms of my hands, my back. And so it went. I never said no. After all that kissing, we made love. It was different from anything I had experienced in those games. I had enjoyed the kissing, but in the act itself, I did not feel anything. She told me my whole body would vibrate, that I would feel dizzy, and go to another world. But I felt none of that. In any case, my "teacher" thus became my teacher for kissing and sexual loving. Since then, during the past thirty-three years, I have realized that she was an expert in kissing and sex. I almost always remember her when I am making love with others and I must say that it would be difficult for anybody to surpass her.

The next day in class, my teacher started to stare at me during recess and told me I could not go out to play. She started to get jealous of me and of the little girls who sent me love notes. Finally, she totally forbade me to go outside for recess. We spent a whole year like that.

By the time I turned twelve, my voice had started to change and my teacher often said to me, "You are my husband. When you are a little older, we will marry. I am in love with you, not with all these young men who are in love with me. I don't know what is happening to me. You are too young but you are a real man."

Around that time I finally felt the nervous ecstasy of which she had spoken. It was a Sunday morning. There was no class. For the first time, I went to that other world and came to know love as a precious divine gift between man and woman.

Later I experienced this relationship as something shameful. Many of my little friends knew that something was going on. My mother must have known, too, because she scolded me a lot and was not as nice to the teacher as before. I did not understand my shame, but it pushed me to want to leave Awastara. I was also concerned about continuing my education, which I clearly could not do in that situation. So I confided my situation to a man who was the husband of one of my aunts. He was about to leave for the gold mines at Bonanza, and I asked him to take me with him. He said he had only enough money for his own trip, so I stole my mother's horse and rode it to Puerto Cabezas, where I sold it for ninety cordobas. With that money I bought a plane ticket to Bonanza. I did what I believed I had to do. When I left home, I felt scared and sad, but hopeful that I had made the best decision. It was with a pain in my heart that I went to live in Bonanza, about 160 miles southwest of Awastara. But on that day of my life I started to become a man.

Some months later, after I had earned some money, I returned to Puerto Cabezas, where I bought back the horse and returned it to mother. She told me she would have let me sell it if I had just asked her.

I did not see that teacher again until some twelve years later, when she was a middle-aged woman and I was a grown man. We greeted each other very cordially and respectfully. She wanted to reinitiate the liaison, but I told her I could not go back to something that had already passed. I loved her, but I was more interested in my relations with women my own age.

Now that I am a mature man, I can look back on that part of my young life and genuinely appreciate certain relationships that I took for granted then. I remember especially the times I shared with my paternal grandfather, Kleofas Reyes, who was born in Awastara and lived there until he died, in 1974. As far as I know, grandfather was a religious man and was considered a governor—a *kasiki* (in Miskito) or *cacique* (in Spanish)— that is, the leader of the Indians living in our little village. He had good connections with the government, always demonstrating an ability to make the correct arrangements in order to assist our people with their problems and dealings with the Somozan authorities.

Kleofas owned lots of horses and cows and had many coconut palms, but he was not considered a rich man by any means. He was married to my grandmother, Elena, a light-skinned Miskito woman, but Grandfather had a certain notoriety for enjoying the company of young girls.

Kleofas loved horses. He was like a cowboy who lived to ride spirited horses and make love with lots of young ladies. Grandfather did not fight, drink, or mistreat anyone, but he did love to make romance with the maidens of Awastara.

I used to go around to see him when I was a small boy of eight or nine. I remember that he often took me out into the bush to hunt deer. Kleofas had a reputation for being a good hunter. When he went hunting for deer, I would follow behind, learning his ways of tracking game and using a gun. I had two guns, a .22-caliber long rifle and a 20-gauge shotgun, one of which I would carry but never fire when I went with Grandfather. I would just follow him and watch what he did.

My admiration for my grandfather grew by leaps and bounds until I got to believing that he could never make a mistake or disappoint me . As far as I was concerned he was nothing less than a noble genius. There was always a spirit of adventure when we hoisted the sail on his big canoe. Whether hunting in the bush or placing nets for fish, my grandfather always applied a keen strategy to the task, which more often than not resulted in fresh game or fish for the dinner table. If the catch was small or the kill not realized, Grandfather would study his tactics to find what had gone wrong. I marveled at this man who was bigger than life.

Then one night—I clearly remember—I made an enlightening journey into the bush with Grandfather. I was seven then. Late in the night we walked ever so quietly into the bush to hunt deer. We used a flashlight to spot the animal. I held the light on the first deer we saw, which seemed to be about a hundred yards away, while my grandfather took aim and fired. The deer ran. I knew that the bullet never struck the deer, but I said nothing. About half an hour later we heard another deer, and again I held the light steady as Grandfather fired twice. The deer ran. Grandfather scratched his head in bewilderment and seemed a bit embarrassed, so I kept quiet. We spotted a third deer, and Grandfather fired a blast down the beam of light I had fastened to the target. Quickly I asked, "Do you think you shot him?" And my grandfather said emphatically, "Yes. I'm sure I shot him. I sure think I hit this one. Well, let's go see the deer."

When we arrived at the spot, there was no deer and no evidence that the bullet had struck the animal. I told Grandfather that the bullet had missed, that it had gone over the deer. I said, "I saw that bullet come out of your gun and pass over the top of the deer. It never touched him."

We kept on walking as Grandfather pretended to look for evidence of a hit. After a few more minutes, he said to me, "You sure you saw the bullet? Let's talk about that." So we sat down together in the bush with the still black of the night around us. I was quiet. Then Grandfather said, "I know very well that when a gun goes off, nobody can see the bullet, because it goes too fast. So how did you see it?"

I looked right at him and spoke the truth, "The bullet must have gone over the deer because there is no other explanation. That bullet never touched the deer!"

I had made up that story about seeing the bullet leave the gun because Grandfather had told me a lie when he said, "I'm sure I shot it." He knew full well that the bullet never touched the animal. I protested against Grandfather telling the lie and insisted that we go home.

The lessons that I learned from my grandfather were invaluable, although it is only now that I am able to judge the usefulness of those strong impressions. Whether engaged as a warrior, a comandante, a parent, a high sport, or a grandfather, which I myself have been for four years now,* I can sense a portion of my grandfather Kleofas in myself.

After I left Awastara at thirteen, I saw grandfather only occasionally. When I was fifteen I went to El Salvador to study, and upon my return to Nicaragua three years later I lived in Sandy Bay for a year. Then I moved to Managua.

Grandfather died in 1974. It was just about that time that I began to be involved with the revolution. In the years since, I have brought a certain amount of honor to my family in Awastara, and I suspect that grandfather Kleofas would have been proud of my accomplishments and my missions on behalf of our people. I have to believe that when my people sing in my honor a Miskito folk song that describes the ways of the tiniska hummingbird, grandfather's joyful pride surely spills over the edges of heaven. The lyrics of that song speak of a fast-flying little bird who flits among the bush and woodlands, sucking sweet nectar from only the prettiest flowers.

---

*Names and approximate ages (as of 1988) of Reynaldo Reyes's grandchildren, who are the children of Marisol Reyes Mejia (Reyes oldest daughter) and Reynaldo Segura:

Kilder Segura Reyes	M	4	
Micci Segura Reyes	F	3	
Jimmy Segura Reyes	M	18	months

Three / Yopta

With a Pain in My Heart

The struggle to become educated began for me at the age of five when I encountered a bad rule. But that was a small obstacle compared to the forces of reality that I faced alone at the age of thirteen in the town of Bonanza. I had neither family nor friend to help me, nor did I have money or a place to live.

I went to the Neptune Gold Mining Company to apply for work. My first job was getting sand out of big tanks after a mercury process had gotten the last bits of gold out of it. I worked with a shovel from seven to three in the heat. An angry Jamaican lashed at us with his tongue, saying, "No talking. Talk is for the jail. Today is for work." I had struggled to get that job and I didn't want to lose it, so I killed myself working. Later I was given a little job as an office boy in a place we called the *plantel*. It was just a tiny job that paid me barely enough wages so that I could rent a small room and buy a little food each day. I was proud of my little job, though, and worked hard. I hoped eventually to get a work schedule that would permit me to attend school with the other children in Bonanza. But my employer continued to increase my work hours, and I did not dare complain. I had to have that little job or I would not have been able to provide for myself.

I was always imagining the day when I would begin school again. As my workdays grew longer, I agonized over my difficulties so much that when I did have time to sleep I could not, because my mind was on studying. I did not rest well at night, and yet I was expected to work longer hours each passing day.

Every morning as I walked to work to make my living, I took notice of the boys and girls on their way to school. The pain in my heart grew larger with each realization of the facts of my young life, which prevented me from joining the others in the classroom. I think I would have surely perished in this dilemma if Mistress Elena had not rescued me.

Doña Elena was a married Spanish lady of about twenty-five years of age who lived in a house near my quarters. She had observed my wistful glances toward the town children on their way to school and had engaged me in conversation on several occasions when I passed by her house, which was on my way to the Neptune Gold Mining Company. She took a sincere interest in me and over the months came to know me and to understand the trouble I was passing through. For nearly a year I had struggled with long hours of work and unrealized goals.

When I was fourteen this kind woman offered to help me solve my problems. She invited me to live in her house, for which I paid her a very small rent. Each day she found food for me to eat and prepared my meals. I then had smaller financial responsibilities and was able to reduce my work hours so that I had time in the afternoons to attend school.

The pain in my heart eased now that I had a friend to assist me. Doña Elena helped me with my studies and gave me the moral support I needed. Through her kindness I was able to complete grades five and six in the town of Bonanza, graduating from elementary school when I was fifteen.

After graduation I quit my job at the mine and went home to Awastara. Only twice since leaving at thirteen had I been back to visit my family. On those two occasions I had been approached by some religious people from the Church of God in Awastara who had expressed a desire to know more about me and my program of study in Bonanza. Now, all Miskitos are born into the Moravian faith. I had gone to church meetings by habit, and when I left the meetings I was still ready to go and find the girl who said she wanted to meet me in the dark. The Moravian pastors smoked, so the members did, too. We were lax in our faith in many ways. The Church of God was a new mission in our region, with harsher discipline: no smoking, no dancing, no sex. The missionaries spoke with me in particular because I seemed to be a modest and honest young man who had the calling to be a leader. After talking with them for a few months and studying the Bible, I accepted their discipline and was baptized. Some thirty or forty others in Awastara joined, including my mother and most of my family.

During the time I had been away from home, these Church of God missionaries, with financial help from their headquarters in Cleveland, Tennessee, had procured a scholarship for me to attend an evangelical school of religion in Santa Tecla, El Salvador.

I was receptive to this idea and grateful for the opportunity to continue studying, even though I realized at the time that the program would be limited to studies of theology and the Bible. The missionaries asked that I return their favor by coming back to the Atlantic Coast to pastor a church after completing the seminary program.

Now I can see that at the age of fifteen I did not have the necessary depth of character to make such a promise, but at the time I honestly believed that I possessed the qualities required by the profession. So I went to El Salvador to study for three years at the Instituto Biblico Centroamericano (Central American Bible Institute).

Gabino H. de Castillo, a Guatemalan, was the director of the school, and his wife, Christina, an American, functioned as second director. I believe that Christina de Castillo is still living today. During my three years at the institute I pursued my studies with great energy and dedication. I learned how to write sermons, how to speak and use gestures to capture an audience. And, of course, I studied the Scriptures and learned how to interpret them according to the teachings of the Church of God. All of this course work was in Spanish, so I had the double difficulty of having to study new subjects while learning a new language.

I was feeling lonely for my home village and for my mother. It was not possible for me to return to Nicaragua for even one visit with my mother during that period of my life. Because there was no way to send mail or even messages by telegraph, I was unable to communicate with my mother even once from the time I was fifteen until I was eighteen.

In my eighteenth year I graduated from the Instituto Biblico Centroamericano, receiving a diploma and full accreditation as a minister of the Church of God. There was a great celebration given in my honor when I returned home to Awastara. The confidence in me demonstrated by my village gave me the courage to fill the pulpit of the Church of God at Sandy Bay. But there was no church, no pulpit, and no members there. It was my mission to go to Sandy Bay and create all of those things. At that particular time in Northern Zelaya there were three Church of God ministers. In Awastara was a minister named Joel Mercado; in Puerto Cabezas Ronaldo Collins was helping to organize a congregation; and a Spanish woman named Socorro Perfino flew from Managua to the Atlantic Coast on occasion to engage in evangelistic work in the Indian communities.

When I first went to Sandy Bay, I was a stranger. There were many children in the community in need of education, but we had no building and no educational materials other than the schoolbooks I had collected over the years, including those from my early days in Awastara and Bonanza. Determined to succeed, I began by making friends among the children. First, I organized a baseball team, and we played ball every moment that the sun was in the sky. After several weeks had passed by and I had made good friends with many of the young boys, I suggested that we, the baseball team, build a schoolhouse. With help from those young friends, I built a twenty-two-by-twenty-six-foot building. The sides we made of pine, and the roof of palm. We had no chairs and no desks, but we had twenty-five students, both boys and girls. I began to teach classes Monday through Friday using all of my old books, then some months later I went to Managua to buy other materials. The children studied mathematics, language, history, geography, and religion. Of course, there was much exercise in the form of baseball.

None of the children in Sandy Bay could read or write when

we began the project, but many were smart and quick to learn. Two boys I remember well from that group of students were William Flores, who was seven, and Charli Rayos, fifteen. These two boys learned quickly, and I could see in them great promise. I have been told recently that these two former students of mine have done well in their lives. William Flores, after finishing his education on the coast, went on to study at the National Autonomous University (UNAN) in Managua, then later went to the United States to study engineering. I believe that now he is living in the United States and working at his profession. The other boy, Charli Rayos, went to Puerto Cabezas when he was in his twenties, where he was given a job in the Moravian hospital. For four years he studied with the doctors in the hospital, learning how to do surgery and deliver babies. Now he is in Sandy Bay working as a paramedic. One year ago, while I was in Sandy Bay, I saw Charli and was happy to see the good work he is doing for our people. He is the principal medical practitioner for that community now.

That year that we had the first schooling in Sandy Bay, I taught the children day and night. They were as starved for education as I had been in Awastara. On Sundays we would use the school building for church services. On the first Sunday that I led a religious service, there was but one family in attendance, that of my student William Flores. Today the church membership is large, and more buildings have been constructed. In that first year I laid a good foundation in Sandy Bay for the Church of God.

When I went to Sandy Bay on my mission for the church, I had been studying for six continuous years. Suddenly I found myself not studying anymore, and I became painfully aware of that nearly forgotten but intense feeling of emptiness in my life. All kinds of new ideas and opinions began to fill up the spaces of my mind. I felt a great need to develop and refine those ideas, most of which were not related in the least to the profession to which I had become attached.

Just a young man of nineteen years, I was trying hard to fulfill my obligation to the church in Sandy Bay. But I was frustrated and restless. There was a young girl in that community who became important to me at that time in my life. She was fourteen years old. I found a comforting refuge in her arms and good friendship in her company. It was in that bloom of youthful companionship that I committed adultery with this young maiden and found myself a participant in the "ways of sin" that I was opposing each Sunday from the pulpit. The contradiction was incompatible with my conscience. I confessed the "sin" to the elders of the church, and we mutually agreed that I would leave Sandy Bay.

I felt ashamed that I had not been able to fulfill my promise to the missionaries and to the church. I had tried my best, but I was not equal to the task. I had concluded that pastoring a church was not the correct profession for me at that period in my life. Besides, I had some vague notion that I had an important role in life to fulfill and this had not been it. That idea of having a special purpose in life began nibbling at my soul.

I knew that I had been happiest when I was studying, so I went to Managua on the Pacific Coast to continue my education, which I believed would help me to become that person in my future who would make an honorable contribution to society. At that time I had no specific idea of what my role would be. I suppose that history had not caught up with my life or maybe I had not caught up with history. It is difficult to judge such things when you are immersed in them. In retrospect, I can see that timing had a great significance in that I happened to be living in Managua just when the revolution was being born in the minds and hearts of the people who lived there. These were unfamiliar ideas to me.

During my life spent in eastern Nicaragua, I had never been very much concerned with politics. The Indians had been ignored by Somoza as a general rule and in Awastara we hardly ever projected our thoughts beyond our own lakes, rivers, and pine forests. If there had been any problems involving the government authorities, the *kasiki* handled it without involving the people. Therefore, I had no direct experience in the political arena. But when I later went to live in Managua, I saw and felt for the first time in my life direct political oppression. I could feel this powerful idea of revolution creeping all around me, seeping through the cracks of the shanties in the ghettos, and filling the hearts and minds of these poor, poor people with hope of a better way of life.

It was very hard to find work that year in Managua, but I did get a job as an inspector who made trips into the countryside to check on the health clinics where antimalarial medicine was being given to the campesinos. With some friends, I had taken a course on malaria and its transmission, then had to take a test. I was still having difficulty with Spanish, so people teased me, saying I would never pass the test, but I did. It was my job to see that there were adequate amounts of medicine and to evaluate the medical personnel and the process of distribution. Also, I was responsible for recording the health statistics of the people who had received the medicine. It was a big job that required many hours of work and travel each day.

Just like in Bonanza years before, I was alone in a strange place wanting to begin school again but having to work at my job every day instead. I began saving a little money for the day I could return to my studies. Then I met a beautiful Spanish girl named Magda.

Magda was sixteen years old when we met and fell in love. Because of my "sin" in Sandy Bay, I could not marry Magda in the church. The church prohibited me from marrying anyone other than the first person with whom I had a sexual relation. That is the law and the discipline of the church to which I had agreed and with which I felt obligated to abide. But I loved Magda and desperately wanted a companion, so we made a home together and cared for one another in an attitude of complete respect as husband and wife. We did not feel that our union was denigrated in any way by the fact that it had not been blessed by the church.

With the birth of our first child—a girl—in 1970, I was jolted by the reality of what lay ahead. If I was ever going to return to my studies I would just have to do it now whether or not I could see a way to afford both an education and a family.

I began school again, at the tenth-grade level, and the babies kept coming. It seemed as though my passing to the next highest grade always brought with it the birth of a new baby.* Only by the grace of God did I manage my studies, my job, my Magda, and five beautiful children, four girls and one boy. After passing through grades ten through twelve, I graduated from Colegio El Maestro in 1973 at the age of thirty.

It was after graduation that I had time to reflect on my long struggle with learning. I wanted to make things easier for other Miskito boys wishing to become educated, so I made a personal commitment to help those young Miskito boys on the Atlantic Coast to get an education in Managua, where I could assist them financially and provide them a place to live. My own struggle had been so painful and so long. I believed that if I could give direct assistance to my young Miskito boys, then perhaps they could get the education they needed without having to suffer as I had suffered.

In 1974 I began making trips to the Atlantic Coast, bringing back to Managua those young boys who wanted to study. Magda felt inconvenienced by these boys living in our house. She never did like it when I made those trips to Puerto Cabezas, and eventually she became discontented.

I continued this routine, hoping that my Magda would learn to appreciate and understand just how hard it was for my Indian people to receive an education. We always had three or four Miskito boys living in our house in Managua while they attended school. But Magda never did come to understand the importance of this, and she began to argue constantly with me about the inconvenience of having those boys in our household.

I understood that this arrangement required more work of Magda and allowed the two of us less time together, but I was willing to make this sacrifice and adamant about the rightness of my decision to help my boys.

*Names and approximate ages (as of 1988) of children born to Reynaldo Reyes and Magda Mejia:

Marisol Reyes Mejia	F	18
Mariluz Reyes Mejia	F	16
Magdaly Reyes Mejia	F	15
Lester Reyes Mejia	M	12
Marileen (Lena) Reyes Mejia	F	11

As the weeks and months passed, Magda grew more and more bitter until she became so dissatisfied with our life together that she gave me an ultimatum: "Your Miskito people or me!"

I knew that if my Magda left, our children would be put at a distance from me, and that probable outcome was offensive to me in every way. So I tried to appease my wife by staying in Managua and limiting my travels with my boys.

Our oldest daughter, Marisol, who was nine or ten years old at that time, was fully aware of the long-standing disagreement between her mother and me over this issue of my participation in the education of my Miskito boys. Even this young girl could understand my intense feelings for my people and would plead with her mother to comprehend. Magda did understand to a great degree; she continued to help my boys, washing their clothes and preparing their meals, and is still remembered fondly for her generosity. Finally, however, the quality of my relationship with Magda had deteriorated to such a degree that everyone in the family was suffering. Marisol's pleas to her mother to "care for Papa, love him and follow him whenever he needs you" fell on an unsympathetic heart. Magda left, taking the children with her, to live many miles from Managua in the town of Chontales, where her mother was living.

WORKING WITH THE SANDINISTAS

I became familiar with the aims of the Sandinistas during business travels I made during the time I was with Magda. Here I need to backtrack a bit. Magda and I had worked for the Olympic shoe company; I sold shoes for them. I eventually went into business for myself selling shoes. With about $130 we had saved up, I bought a bunch of shoes to sell in other towns outside Managua. I made about 80 percent profit in three days and returned with my pocket full of orders. I made several more trips. In two weeks I made what I made in five months in the shoe factory. Magda asked for a leave and then quit her job, and we traveled all over Nicaragua, even to Bluefields, on the southern Atlantic Coast. I eventually bought a big Daihatsu truck from the owner of the Olympic shoe factory. I filled it with shoes that the factories let me take on confidence. With the money I made, we bought a farm in the Zone of New Guinea.

In 1976 I met a tall, slender Sandinista man of about twenty-three years of age named Mario. A traveling merchant in the region, he was also a young revolutionary engaged in securing weapons for the guerrillas. Mario explained how the Indians had been marginalized; how the oligarchy was in control; how the youth were gaining the faith of Sandino (1893–1934), the general of the poor, a nationalist who had been against exploitation by imperialist transnational companies; how the poor had only sickness and poverty to show for the presence of the foreigners; how the products of Nicaragua should be for Nicaraguans first; how only surplus products should be exported. I was already convinced of all of this by my own experience. These were all truths about our marginality and exploitation as Indians. So I began buying pistols, rifles, clothes, and boots with my own money, and I talked friends into donating as well.

There was no work at the time, so I decided to fight for liberty and change, to get rid of oppression. Magda had told me the revolution was for those who did not have families to support, and that Somoza would never lose. I disobeyed her and went into the mountains near Matagalpa, north of Managua, in the first months of 1976. We spent two months without fighting, avoiding confrontations, just training politically and physically. Finally our group of thirteen guerrillas ambushed a military truck. We didn't do it very well. They counterattacked and we fought for half an hour before retreating. Two Somocistas died. I noticed from their eyes how scared my inexperienced compañeros were. The young squad leader was only eighteen.

Later we went to Río Blanco and joined a group of twenty-five others. We had problems with food, organization, and a lack of support from the campesinos. Some would report us to the Guardia. The ones who liked us called us the *muchachos*. I was patient with the Spanish youths because I understood that they were university kids who had gone from the classroom, the cinema, and the stadium to the jungle. They tired easily and did not carry their weapons right. We managed no more than an ambush or two a month. I spent a year like that. They called me "el Indio" (the Indian).

Then, in March 1978, I was sent to Cuba for three months. I first learned the history of the guerrilla struggle, starting three thousand years before Christ. In China there was a guerrilla who fought with his men against the fragmented monarchies that were exploiting their subjects and making them pay heavy tribute. He raised his people's consciousness and taught them to make weapons from the bones of animals and sticks. He liberated his people from their oppression. I also remember that they told us about how when Napoleon arrived in Spain with thousands of soldiers, the inhabitants learned how to ambush rather than fight in frontal attacks, chipping away at Napoleon's forces. Their strategy was called Operation Gas: you can smell gas but cannot see its source. Then we learned of Mao Tse-tung's strategies. Before Mao, people thought one needed a lot of money to make a war. But Mao taught that one should first gain the favor of the masses; second, know the terrain; third, make weapons yourself or receive them from the people; and finally, seek money to buy weapons. Those weapons would be held with greater love because of the sense of representing the people. This way the revolutionary army does not depend on money. It can innovate and continue the struggle. We also learned to make weapons and bombs, how to cross rivers, train physically, and communicate in codes by radio.

We learned the strategy of the ambush. First, you have to look for the place to which you will retreat after the attack, a safe place to regroup. Second, find the place to attack from. Third, make sure the enemy gets confused when the first grenades and shots go off. This confusion needs to be taken advantage of to achieve maximum destruction. This can be done best on a slope or on a bridge. The radio operator and the drivers of the vehicles are the most important targets.

The Cubans treated us with friendship and respect, but also with discipline. In discussions outside of training, they always tried not to lose time and kept to serious topics.

When they sent us back to Nicaragua, there were about ten Nicaraguans, two Hondurans, and five Cubans on the plane. We flew very low over the water as soon as we got into Nicaraguan airspace to avoid detection. I was scared to death that I was going to drown before I could die for the revolution. We flew over Sandy Bay, and later the plane made a big swing, landed near Chontales, and let us off with our weapons. We all felt empowered, ready to fight and ready to teach the compañeros in Nicaragua. I personally belonged to the eastern front, where Luis Carrion was the commanding officer.

Our orders were to go ahead and fight. In charge of roughly thirty-five men, I made frequent ambushes and attacks against Somoza's National Guard. Once we came close to Juigalpa, a few miles out, and arrived at a farm late in the afternoon. The owner was not there, but the workers gave us a lot of food and treated us well. The campesinos were already much more on our side by then. We didn't let anybody leave to avoid being discovered. The owner was supposed to come back the next morning. He was a rich man who knew a lot about the movement of Somoza's troops. He promised me he would deliver information and went into town. Much later in the day, the owner came back and told me that there was group of Somocistas fixing a truck in nearby Las Palmas. He told us he would take us over there in a truck. We thought he must be a Somocista, so we made him ride in the truck with us in case he was trying to set us up.

We got about two miles outside Las Palmas and waited all night, not letting the farm owner go. We began to doubt his information, but I decided to stick it out. Finally, three trucks full of guardsmen came down the road toward us. I had to change strategy quickly. I spread out my men in three groups into positions where the trucks would stop in a row. It was a perfect ambush. We shot the tires and drivers first and then nearly exterminated the whole group of about twenty or thirty soldiers per truck. They were low on ammunition and could not defend themselves at all well. They had already passed through a number of attempts to attack them and only had sixty miles to go to get to Managua. A group of our comrades up the road had given up on waiting for the convoy, so people commented later about how the "Indio" had waited patiently all through the night.

Another episode in 1977 found us outside Villa Somoza, where Magda was living with our children and her mother. I had good information about the town and knew exactly where the command post was. We encircled it at about eight in the morning. There were about ten guardsmen there. They had captured four boys who had been helping us and were going to send them to Managua. We went to free them and started shooting. As two guardsmen were entering the command post, we shot them from behind, then while one of them was shouting and moaning, "They shot me, those sons of bitches," I had four men ready to get the boys out of the jail inside. The guardsmen ran and jumped out the window, and the towns-people shouted, "The *muchachos* are here!" We freed the boys, and the townspeople thought the revolution had arrived. About twenty-five new boys joined us that day and we got weapons for them at a big store run by a Somocista named Peralta.

I did not see my family except for a brief visit upon my return from Cuba. Magda probably believed I was dead. I missed my family a lot during those days, but my love for liberty was greater, because especially for me, the Somoza administration was a yoke and a burden. Even though my business was doing fine, I wanted liberty for everyone. I knew that my children and Magda were suffering from the possibility that I could die any day and they would be left alone. I was sad at these thoughts and often wondered whether I could really change the world, but I dismissed such thoughts as temptations that would distract me from my task. It helped a lot when the masses started to support our cause. Furthermore, I could not imagine abandoning my comrades in the mountains. A man cannot live beneath the control of another man, I thought. The people have to be free, so I have to fight for the revolution, even if the people do not understand what we were fighting for. I remember something that Che Guevara said, something about the man who stays with the struggle until the last moment being the true man.

By 1978 the support for the Sandinista guerrilla was profound. The campesinos willingly gave us their last bits of food, even taking it out of the mouths of their children. When the National Guard started to shoot peasants for cooperating, the younger peasant boys would then join the struggle, even without weapons. It strengthened me to see their courage and their strong desire for liberty.

Big strikes were starting. The workers were burning factories and tires in the streets. Somoza's air force started to bomb certain barrios in Managua where there were young people who might join the revolution. Pedro Joaquín Chamorro had been assassinated on January 10, 1978. We could smell victory. We had a lot more men than we could arm. Those without arms cooperated as best they could. The comandante Luis Carrion worked hard to politicize the youth as they joined and to explain to them what the struggle was all about.

We kept hitting the National Guard hard here and there. They started attacking us more from the air. We had some sharpshooters with Super-FALs (Belgian assault rifles) and RPG-2s (Soviet grenade launchers) posted on the peaks of the hills to shoot at planes, but the planes never came low enough. We began to lose fear and sensed the coming triumph.

In 1979 I remember especially entering Juigalpa, where my sister Karolina and her husband took care of the zoo. I spoke with her and found out some things about how the National Guard was operating locally and about our support among the people. She knew a lot because she had traveled selling electrical appliances. Thirty-two or so of my men were camped out in a place where she said the Guard never came. We spent a night and day there, then left, staying near the city. We didn't have enough information to strike the command post in town, so I had the idea of going to sell appliances around town, to enter the post and see what was going on. We forgot about the idea for a while and had skirmishes here and there in the area. When I shared my idea with the boys, they forbade me to do it. Finally my sister offered to go and find out, so she went to the command post, entered the kitchen, and got the idea of asking the cook how many tortillas they made for each meal. The cook revealed the information and we were able to calculate that there were no more than two hundred men there. We were able to plan a combined attack with two hundred of our own men a few days before the Triumph, on July 16. The city of Juigalpa was under siege by then, since our forces occupied the hills near the town. Luis Carrion and other co-mandantes attacked with us at four in the morning.

The guardsmen stayed inside the buildings mostly, but some went out to the roof-tops. We had sharpshooters posted all over town to pick them off. A few women wrapped in shawls would walk along crying, then pull out a pistol and shoot a passing guardsman, then go on crying. It was a big mess. Everyone in the town was screaming and shouting. The same things were happening in Estelí, Matagalpa, and León.

We chased the guardsmen as if we were chasing rabbits. We fought through the morning and occupied all the high spots. The colonel tried to escape with his family in a helicopter. We managed to hit it, and it fell into the bush nearby. Twenty prisoners were freed from the jail. Some of the guardsmen were allowed to escape, but many were shot upon surrendering. By one in the afternoon, we had taken the command post. The *muchachos* were regarded as angels from heaven. The stores were all opened, and food was given out to hungry people.

After that, I was among eighty chosen to go into Managua, where we were posted along the road to the airport to stop the many trucks full of Somocista guardsmen trying to flee to Honduras. I often wondered in those hours about my mother's brother who was in the Guard. I thought he was in Managua, and every time I saw a corpse I checked to see if it was him. Later I learned that he had been a lieutenant in the navy based in Bluefields, and had left for Honduras when Somoza fell.

AFTER THE TRIUMPH

In August 1979 the Sandinistas sent me to Bluefields. My mission was to disarm a group of anti-Sandinistas who were led by a Creole man named Abel. This anti-Sandinista group worked on a large agricultural cooperative and took over the palace and the government meetinghouse in Bluefields. Abel wanted to control Bluefields. Feeling identified with the Sandinistas at that time, as most of us did, Abel's rebellion seemed wrong to me. I aligned myself with a Miskito named Bobi Holmes, a Creole named Lumberta Campbell, and a woman named Leana Benavides. Then we began our political work in the community of Bluefields to stop the fight against the new government. When that mission was completed, the Sandinistas sent me back to Managua for a short while, then flew me to a Río Coco community called Waspam, on Nicaragua's northern border.

In that community a Spanish Sandinista big man called Cesar-3 was killing people who had had close connections with the Somozan government. A Miskito by the name of Eduardo Moody, who had been Somoza's agent in the town of Bihmuna, was then in jail in Waspam. At three A.M. one night Cesar-3 went to the jail to kill Moody, but I confronted him, saying, "You cannot kill him! The Triumph is not reason enough to exterminate people." The Sandinista soldiers backed me up, and Cesar-3 did not kill Moody as he had planned. A few days later the government sent me to Puerto Cabezas, where I remained for a short while before returning to Managua.

With Somoza in exile and the new government of the Sandinistas in place in Managua, the country began to try to organize itself. On the Atlantic Coast neither the government nor the army was organized. Historically the Spanish had not been involved there to any degree, so their presence and influence was weak, especially in Northern Zelaya, where Puerto Cabezas was the largest community.

Comandante Rene Vivas from the Ministry of the Interior sent me to work on the Atlantic Coast to help organize Tropa Guarda Frontera (TGF), the Sandinista military organization that defended the border with Honduras to the north and the northern Atlantic coastline. My base was in the community of Tronquera, a small town north of Puerto Cabezas, where I functioned as chief communications officer and paymaster for the Sandinista government. The government began moving troops into the border communities of Cabo Gracias a Dios, Bom (Boon), Waspam, Kum, Bilwaskarma, Leimus, San Alberto, and San Carlos; also, into the coastal communities of Bihmuna, Sandy Bay, and Puerto Isabel. Many of the Miskito Indians joined the troops defending these borders because all of us wanted to protect the freedom that had been won in the Triumph. It was about this time that we the Miskito people began to collaborate with the new government to organize MISURASATA (*Miskito, Sumo, Rama, Sandinista, aslaTakan* [United Together]).

MISURASATA developed many projects to enhance the quality of life for the people living on the Atlantic Coast. One of the first projects was a literacy campaign, which we called *campaña de alfabetización*. I encouraged our Miskito people to participate in the campaign because I knew the importance of education and believed that this would benefit all of us. I asked for a leave from the military to take part personally in this effort.

Those people from all ethnic groups who knew how to read and write taught those who did not. I felt grateful to the Sandinista government, then and now, for having made this possible. Also, MISURASATA allowed us for the first time in history to be truly organized throughout the Atlantic Coast. All of the Indian tribes experienced a renewal of friendship and motivation to work together for the betterment of all of the Indian peoples of Nicaragua.

Before the Triumph, we had only one Indian organization, AL PROMISO, which was founded in 1973. But AL PROMISO had never fully developed because it had no support from the Somoza government. That government had believed the organization to be their opponent, and a rivalry had developed out of that belief. Moreover, the Somoza government had used some Miskitos—Alba Rivera and Adolfo Bushy—as civil servants on the Atlantic Coast. After the Triumph, these elected officials were of no use to the Miskito people and could not function in any productive way with the Sandinistas because of their former ties to Somoza. It was with the help of my companions and a commander of the republic that we arranged for Comandante Daniel Ortega to come to Puerto Cabezas on two occasions to speak about the necessity for us to work together with the new government so that programs to enhance the quality of our lives could be carried out. It was after this second visit that MISURASATA was formed and began to function in a way that was pleasing to the Miskito and to the Sandinista government.

The good relations between my people and the Sandinista government for several months following the Triumph were due in large part to the effectiveness of MISURASATA, which was led by Steadman Fagoth, who was part Miskito and part German (through Moravian missionaries).

Fagoth went around saying that he was a Sandinista guerrilla who had fought in the West, but he was soon discovered to be a fraud and was kicked out of the Sandinista police. Nevertheless, he was perceived as well educated, a model for his people, guiding them toward a good future, and revealing their exploitation by the transnational companies. I saw him as an opportunist, more fantasy than reality, an egocentric sweet-talker who was upset because he was not able to hold key posts with the Sandinistas. He satisfied his yearnings by becoming chief of MISURASATA. My people, who had been without a leader for a hundred years, welcomed him.

Fagoth quickly gained the respect of our people during this first productive phase of the organization. Good relations lasted until 1980. Up until that time, we did not have any particular opinion about this new government's policy of "socialism." We only knew that life was better for us and that the Cuban doctors sent to replace our Atlantic Coast doctors, who had fled with their money at the time of the Triumph, were helping our people with their health needs, inoculating our children with vaccines never available to us before, and providing us with services essential to our lives. We did not consider their political persuasions because, in reality, this was not a factor in their involvement in our community. They were not "politically active." They just did their jobs, and we were grateful to them and to the Sandinistas for having sent them to us.

But this stability was not to last for long. And it was through our organization MISURASATA that the seeds of mistrust of the Sandinista government were planted and cultivated in the minds of the Miskito people.

Four / Walhwal

1980–1981: A New Leader for the Miskitos

In 1980 Steadman Fagoth, along with two other Miskito leaders, Hazel Law and Brooklyn Rivera, began holding secret meetings in Puerto Cabezas with the Miskito people. The open MISURASATA meetings continued under his leadership at the same time.

I am not sure what motivated Fagoth initially to rebel against the Sandinista government. That motivation may have come from within himself or it may have come from an outside source such as the CIA. Of course, in the first of these secret meetings Fagoth never mentioned the CIA, which had already begun to seek ways to reverse the Sandinista triumphs; but since that time evidence has been made public that Fagoth's strong ties to the CIA and to the Oficina de la Seguridad Nacional (OSN), Somoza's secret police, dated back to his college days in Managua during the 1970s. Fagoth had used the name "Saul Torrez." A handwritten letter to the OSN signed by Steadman Fagoth, followed by "Saul Torrez" in parentheses, was found in Somoza's files after the Triumph. In that letter Steadman had requested that he be accepted back into the service of the OSN in order to spy on Miskito people who were attending the same university as himself. I never saw that letter with my own eyes, but I did see a copy of it that was published in a Managua newspaper. This evidence was announced after the Sandinistas arrested Fagoth—which makes you wonder why they did not disclose it before Fagoth was made leader of MISURASATA. Perhaps they had not discovered it then. It is always possible for anyone to bring false evidence against someone; I have known Steadman for many years, however, and I do not find it difficult to believe that he would have spied on his own people. He has never demonstrated any real caring for the Miskito people, only caring for himself—the only exception being his organizing the *campaña de alfabetización*. But even that accomplishment was not as grand as it was claimed. It is true that there was a great effort to teach the Indians how to read and write, and it is true that Fagoth deserves a good portion of the credit for that effort. Literate people had to go far up into the mountains and into all kinds of difficult territory to educate the Miskitos. They rode in canoes and on horseback and walked many miles to accomplish the task. But these old Indian people had never been to any kind of school and had never had any experience with an alphabet. I am proud of what my people learned through the efforts of that literacy program, but it was not a great amount that was learned. They were only able to write their names and read just a little. But for that progress, small as it was in reality, I am grateful to MISURA-SATA and to the Sandinistas and to Steadman Fagoth.

It was in the secret meetings with MISURASATA members during 1980 that Fagoth introduced the idea of fighting against the Sandinista government. He insisted that the government was bringing a bad law to Nicaragua—the law of communism—and that this law would eventually incapacitate us as an Indian nation.

I attended many of these secret meetings—skeptical of their correctness and legality, but curious to see for myself what was going on in them. The government had never given me cause to suspect them of insensitivity or gross wrongdoing of the sort described by Fagoth. When he began explaining to us the methods he wanted to use to "overthrow" the Sandinistas, my skepticism grew into a real distrust.

Fagoth told us that the countries of the United States, West Germany, Israel, and Argentina were ready to give assistance to us if we would initiate a war against our government in Managua. If we did not begin this effort now, he said, we would find ourselves at the mercy of "communism."

Fagoth brought to the meetings a book in English that explained how we could make a counterrevolution that would unseat the Sandinistas in two months' time. He had a companion who translated the English text into our language. The book presented examples of other countries where such counterrevolutions had been fought and won. Hazel Law, Brooklyn Rivera, and Steadman Fagoth for many weeks were engaged in this process of convincing our people that they should bring a war against the government.

It was at one of these secret meetings that I asked Fagoth, "With what weapons can we fight against the government?" He said to me, "It is no problem. We are going to make some bows and arrows like they used in ancient days, and we are going to fight with that." Then he told the boys, "Don't worry. Some scientific people are coming from India to throw poison over here to kill out all the Sandinista people, and every night we will be chopping off their heads."

When I looked at him and heard him say those things, I thought to myself, "He is a fool." A man like me is not so easy to fool. I knew better.

Furthermore, I said to Fagoth, "It seems to me, if they throw the poison on the people like that, it will be not only the Sandinistas who will be dead but the Miskito Indians as well. How can this not be so?" Fagoth answered, "Each of the boys will rub a lime and a little salt on himself so he won't be affected by the poison." When he came to this point, I, Ráfaga, said, "No way!"

Fagoth was tricky and clever. He fooled a lot of the boys with these ideas. Nearly all of the MISURASATA boys believed him, but he never did fool me. I never did believe those ideas. From that time until now I have believed that Steadman Fagoth has been an opportunist when given the chance. He only works for personal gain.*

Fagoth knew full well that all the Indians were poorly educated people living in poverty. His motive in trying to persuade

---

*In a November 1991 phone conversation with J. K. Wilson, Ráfaga reported that "Fagoth is working in Managua for the Miskitos in a very good way."

the boys to fight was to get money from the government of the United States. When he initially presented these ideas, in 1980, he had not received any money from the U.S. government—only the promise of money contingent on his ability to recruit Miskito boys to fight the counterrevolution.

My appraisal of Fagoth's ideas was different from the rest of the boys because I had been living in the more sophisticated environment of Managua while getting an education. Not only was I more experienced than the rest, but I also had had access to newspapers in Managua that had kept me informed about the Sandinistas'capabilities of modern warfare. On the Atlantic Coast there are not now nor have there ever been newspapers available to us in our native Indian language. It was easy to see how the boys were charmed by Fagoth's ideas.

Many of the boys followed Fagoth into the bush, where they began making bows and arrows. I did not agree with this. I was against it because Fagoth was brainwashing them from good to bad. That is how it was and how it still is today.

After Fagoth had gotten the boys ready out in the bush, he brought them out from the mountains to fight against the government. There were small, isolated skirmishes with some Sandinista soldiers in Puerto Cabezas and in Prinzapolka, just to the south. The Sandinistas must have thought these Indian boys with their long hair and bows and arrows to be foolish. They did not retaliate in a lethal way—they had no cause in that early time to hurt those foolish boys. Fagoth told the boys that the Sandinistas had not retaliated because they were afraid of the power of the Miskito warriors, and the boys believed what Fagoth said. It was a false pride he put into their minds.

In those days Fagoth used to make a trip each week to Managua on "official" MISURASATA business, believing that the Sandinistas were unaware of his secret counterrevolutionary activities on the Atlantic Coast. But apparently someone had informed the government about the secret meetings. And so it was during one of his trips that the Sandinistas arrested him at the airport in Managua and put him in jail. From his suitcase they confiscated documents and letters that connected him to Somocistas living in Miami, Florida.

There were Atlantic Coast people at the Managua airport that day waiting to board the same plane that Fagoth was to have taken back to Puerto Cabezas. Those people saw him arrested and brought the story back to Puerto Cabezas that same day. The news spread like fire up and down the coast. The next day, a real fight broke out to protest the arrest of the principal leader of the Miskito people. The fight began right in the Moravian church at Prinzapolka. The boys attacked the Sandinistas, not with bows and arrows, but with their bare hands.

I believe that it is really very important for all to know exactly how the real counterrevolutionary war began that day in Prinzapolka. There were many Miskito boys in church that day. Also, two of the Miskito leaders who were close to Fagoth, Elmer Prado and Uriel Zuniga, were there as inspectors of the campaign. Aware of their plans to fight, six Sandinista officers came to the church while services were in progress. They ordered Prado, Zuniga, and eight others to surrender themselves. Two of the Sandinistas stayed at the door while the other four came in to get Prado. None of the Miskito boys nor the leaders had weapons, but when the officers came into the church with their weapons ready, the boys tackled the Sandinistas, eventually took their guns, shot them, then ran into the bush with the government weapons. Three Miskitos died in the fight.

This was a big incident. Government officials were angered by what had happened, but did not retaliate immediately. Instead, the government big man in Puerto Cabezas, Manuel Cheves Calderon, called a meeting of all the ministers and priests, asking them to tell the Miskito boys who were still hiding in the bush to turn themselves and the weapons over to the authorities. Cheves Calderon promised the clergy that no harm would come to the boys if they would return in the way requested. He also promised that if any were hurt in the return that all would be given medical attention. That was a big lie. They had searched all over for those boys and were getting desperate. Prado and Zuniga were both wounded and needed attention, so the elders persuaded them to turn themselves in. When they did, they were beaten and thrown into jail.

At the time this meeting was held, many other Miskito leaders had already been captured and put into jails. The government was trying to defuse Fagoth's idea of bringing a war against the Sandinistas. By removing our leaders, the government believed that the idea would die. But the government's action had an opposite effect on the Indian people. They had been pushed too far and were ready for war.

In that year of 1980, the people began to cross the Río Coco to our Miskito lands in Honduras, especially all of the young boys. I was in Puerto Cabezas at that time.

While Fagoth was in jail in Managua, most of the young Miskito boys went over to Honduras—a whole group of them. I was sad about what had happened to Fagoth because I worried about how they had him in jail. It is true, I never did like his ways or how he spoke foolish lies to the boys, but I respected his right to have an opinion and cared for him physically and spiritually because he is Indian like I am.

Fagoth's father was seriously ill, and the Sandinistas, to show their sympathy toward the family, released Steadman and let him return to Puerto Cabezas so he could visit his parents, who lived north of Port on the Río Coco. Before he left Managua, the government requested he return to Puerto Cabezas after his visit to resume his duties as leader of MISURASATA, and Steadman agreed. When he left the jail, the Sandinistas sent no soldiers or guards with him, but told him, "If you love your people, then you come back to work with them in Puerto Cabezas and with us in Managua."

Fagoth went to his home on the Río Coco, and the very next day he fled across the river to Honduras, where the boys were waiting. I have described these events in order to show you how this Indian was a double-crosser. He did not work in a legal way. He double-crossed our Sandinista government, and that is how the Indian revolution began to organize itself from Honduras.

After Fagoth went to Honduras many, many Miskito people—maybe eight to ten thousand—followed him over because they believed that he was a good leader and a good man. Many Indian leaders also followed Fagoth to join his army.

In Honduras, in 1981, the Indian revolutionaries organized and trained themselves. They received a few weapons from the U.S. government, but most were training with bows and arrows and other crude weapons. Usually only the leaders had good guns and ammunition. It was in that year that Fagoth brought a Christmas shedding of blood to Nicaragua—what came to be known as Navidad Roja, Red Christmas.

One of the key events occurred on the Río Coco at San Carlos, where a troop of Sandinista soldiers were encamped. Vincente Perez, nicknamed "Sutum," was the leader of the Miskito fighters, who called themselves Las Cruces, about eighty men. They came into San Carlos divided into four groups. Most of the warriors had only bows and arrows and rocks as their weapons. They attacked the Sandinista military base at San Carlos, killing every government soldier except the radio operator, whom they captured. When that fight was finished, Sutum and his boys took all the uniforms off the dead soldiers and took their weapons. Then they held a gun to the head of the Sandinista radio operator and forced him to call the government military base at Tronquera to ask the commander there, Lucho Chevarria, to send reinforcements to San Carlos because it was under attack.

Lucho, a Sandinista big man, was about twenty-four years old—a good man, well liked and respected by the Miskito people. When Lucho received the radio message, he and another Sandinista leader, Reynaldo Mendoza, left Tronquera with about fifteen soldiers in a helicopter to fly to San Carlos to reinforce their troops. When the helicopter arrived at San Carlos, Sutum and the Las Cruces Indian fighters were all dressed in Sandinista uniforms. Sutum, looking like a Sandinista, motioned to the helicopter to land, and it did. When Lucho and Mendoza stepped out of the helicopter, Sutum and the boys opened fire on them using the weapons they had taken from the dead Sandinista soldiers. The pilot, along with two soldiers who were wounded but still inside the helicopter, escaped, flying on to Waspam. The copter crashed at Waspam, but those inside survived. Both Sandinista leaders perished. Lucho was found tied to a tree, disemboweled. His heart had been removed. That is how it happened on Christmas Day 1981 at San Carlos. Sutum's second officer gave this history to me. All of this was happening while I was still in Puerto Cabezas working as the chief payroll officer for the Sandinista military.

I never did want to follow Fagoth, nor did I want to leave my Indian people who had remained behind on the Atlantic Coast of Nicaragua. But after Navidad Roja, the Sandinistas became angry with all of the Miskito people because of the death and destruction brought into the country by Fagoth's counterrevolution. The Sandinista soldiers, believing that all of us were in sympathy with Fagoth, began capturing the young Miskito boys living in and around Puerto Cabezas.

They put the Indian boys in jail, beat them up, and executed many of them. Also, the ministers of our churches were captured by the Sandinistas and taken along with the young boys to the prison Zona Franca (called Carcel Modelo during Somozan times) at Tipitapa, near Managua. When these bad things started to happen to our people, many who had not agreed with Fagoth earlier now fled to Honduras because they were afraid of the Sandinistas. Plenty left their homes and their country because of the pressure on them. They were afraid they too would be jailed or killed. They preferred to be in Honduras.

Fagoth called his organization MISURA. He cropped the "SATA" from MISURASATA because those letters signified "*Sandinista asla*Takan" (Sandinista united together [with *Mis*kito, *Su*mo, and *Ra*ma]). Brooklyn Rivera had been released from jail and had gone to Honduras to work with Fagoth. They struggled over power, and Fagoth had Brooklyn put in jail for about fifteen days. Under pressure from several of the Indian officers, Fagoth released him but, assisted by the Honduran military, planned his assassination. So Brooklyn fled to Costa Rica, on Nicaragua's southern border. Fagoth also planned to assassinate Marcos Huffington, from Awastara, and Elmer

Prado (Fagoth's brother-in-law) for challenging his leadership. As a result, Marcos and other leaders followed Brooklyn to Costa Rica, and one year later Fagoth sent his sister and Prado to Miami with their families.

From Costa Rica, Brooklyn organized an Indian fighting force on the southern front. It was agreeable to him to use the MISURASATA name. And so it was that MISURA under the leadership of Fagoth in Honduras and MISURASATA under the leadership of Rivera in Costa Rica brought an Indian revolution against the Sandinistas of Nicaragua. It was about that time that the U.S. government began to support this fight with many good weapons and military supplies, because now two strong Indian leaders were well established on both boundaries with several thousand warriors willing to wage war against a government whose policies and philosophies were in opposition to those of the United States.

Five / Matsip

1981–1982: I Start to Fight

Back before the Navidad Roja, from July 1979 until July 1981, I was a Sandinista commander, functioning as paymaster and chief communications officer at Tronquera, the second-largest base in Northern Zelaya. Lucho Chevarria was the base commander there. I was the only Miskito among the twelve-member *jefetura* and second in charge.

I believe that because I was Miskito, the other officers were distrustful of me and made two serious attempts to frame me so that I would be removed from the *jefetura*. The first attempt came when I received an order from Puerto Cabezas to arrest an eighteen-year-old boy in the Miskito village of Ulwas. I questioned the authority of this order and was told that it had come from a higher authority than Lucho. I knew that for that to be possible a radio message would have been received, and since I had to sign all radio messages personally before they were delivered, I knew that no such message had come to Tronquera. After I refused to go to Ulwas, another Sandinista officer, named Sergio, carried out the mission. The boy was executed. Days later Sergio himself was found floating in the Río Coco. He was buried in the sand near Ulwas. I found out much later that it was the Indians from Ulwas who had killed him.

About a month later there was second attempt to frame me. This time it was the base commander, Lucho, who ordered me to carry out a similar mission. He ordered me to go to Waspam to capture a Miskito woman named Marga Curbelo.

He said I was to take her at two A.M. from her house and bring her to Tronquera. Suspecting that Marga would also be killed, I sent a secret message to her to leave Waspam immediately. She received the message and left for Honduras.

About fifteen days later, on the night of July 1, 1981, while in my quarters at the Sandinista *jefetura* command post, a group of my Sandinista compañeros arrested me and took me to the Tronquera jail. The government believed that all Miskito Indians were participating with MISURA. Because I was Miskito they had begun to mistrust me, and for that they put me in jail. The Sandinista's mistrust of MISURASATA and their opposition to MISURA had developed into a real hatred, which they projected onto all of our people. You had only to be Miskito and that was sufficient cause for them to hate you, put you in jail, or even kill you. They only had to say "You are Miskito!" and you were gone.

I went to jail without resisting them physically. They did not beat me or ill-treat me, but they questioned me extensively. They accused me of having weapons. They asked if I had arms or if I had stolen weapons to give to Fagoth's boys. They said guns and ammunition had been taken from the camp and they believed I was responsible. I told them I knew nothing about the missing weapons. They asked me many more questions and pressured me psychologically by saying they had already caught my comrade in crime, but they released me that same night.

One month later they took me back to jail again. Their reasons were similar to the time before. They accused me of being in contact with the Indian revolutionaries and accused me of collaborating with Fagoth. I told them that this was not true and that, knowing how I felt about Steadman Fagoth, they should realize that it would be absurd for me to collaborate with him. The Sandinistas did not understand this time. They were insensitive and interested only in repression. They were not thinking deeply. This time they did not release me quickly, as they had before. I remained in jail for one full month, then was released.

On November 19, 1981, I was in Puerto Cabezas when the government soldiers put me in jail for the third and final time.* The Sandinista authorities said they had no confidence in me because I was Miskito and because I had refused to accept my wages for my work as paymaster for the past two months. I, in fact, had not been working for them during that time. They wanted to know, "Why don't you want to work like the other Sandinista comandantes?" I simply explained that I could not accept pay for work I did not do. They kept me in the jail without evidence of wrongdoing and without trial.

Six days later, on November 25, I concluded that the Sandinistas were not going to give me my liberty. I was thinking they might kill me or more likely they might send me to a jail in Managua because it was not a popular thing to have me in jail in Puerto Cabezas, where my Miskito people were living all around.

I began that day to exercise my body by walking fast back and forth in the five-by-eight-foot room, and I started to think of ways I might escape. Each day I would walk this way for about sixteen hours.

I had only one visitor while I was in jail. The Sandinistas held me incommunicado, but one day my sister Karolina came to the jail to speak with me and caused such a commotion that the officers brought me down to the office and let me talk with her for about three to five minutes while two soldiers stood guard. Also, two of my children, Magdaly (then age seven) and Lester (age four), would come every day to stand in the street about thirty yards from the front of the jail looking up at the window on the second floor, where I was imprisoned. I never cried out to them, though I could see them well and hear their crying.

The Miskito people on three occasions demonstrated in front of the jail demanding my release. They too were thinking

---

*This jail stood on the site where the Peace Ship/Peace House Construction Brigade, of which J. K. Wilson was a member, would build Casa de la Paz (the House of Peace) in 1987.

that the Sandinistas might try to take me to Managua. They told the officers, "The day we no longer see Reynaldo in the window will be the last day of your lives." On each of those occasions there were one hundred or more protesters. I never called out to my people, but would only stand in the window so they could see me well. I felt like more of a man behaving in this way.

Every day my Indian people would bring food to the jail for me to eat. The guards would accept the food, telling the people that it would be given to me. Then they would eat that good food and give to me only one plate of very old beans each day.

Every one or two days I was taken downstairs to a toilet. That was not a big problem for me, because if there is nothing to eat, there is nothing to shit. It was during one of those trips downstairs that I saw in the toilet bowl a small piece of a Gillette razor, which I retrieved, thinking it might somehow aid me in an escape. When they returned me to my cell, I began to think about cutting the window screen with the razor. But I knew that if I were to do this, I would have to jump out the window and run right at that moment. To cut the screen then wait for a good opportunity to jump would not work, because someone might notice the cut screen while I was waiting, and that would be the end of my escape plan. I had to consider many things in order to plan a successful escape. No one had ever escaped from that jail and lived, although several had tried.

Another important fact I had to consider was that of the Sandinista guard office being located directly beneath my cell. If I did jump from the window, I would be passing by the window of the guard office on the first floor and landing on the ground in full view of anyone in that room.

For many days I was begging God to send a big rain. I believed that in a big storm the guards and soldiers would be less likely to apprehend me. So for days and days I was praying to God to send the rain. When the rain did not come I became very angry with God that He would not help me. Being angry at God made my spirit uncomfortable so much so that on December 17 I made an apology to Him for my willfulness. I was thinking to myself, "If the Sandinistas are going to try to kill me and God is not happy with me, then there is no one to help me."

On the night of December 18 it began to rain. All was quiet beneath me, so I was thinking that the guards might be sleeping. I decided this must be the right time to cut the screen and jump. I went to the window and stretched out my hand to cut it, but my whole arm began to shake. I stopped. "God, help me please," I said. Then after about ten minutes, again I took the Gillette to the window, and again my hand began to tremble. In my spirit I felt uncomfortable, as though God did not agree with my plan. Just in that moment, I looked down on the lawn, where the shadow of a man was moving about in the light that spilled into the yard from the office window. I gave up the plan in a moment, because I had felt sure that the guard was asleep when in truth he was awake. If I had jumped as I had planned, I would have been killed. All night I lay awake on the wood floor thinking of other ways to let the Gillette help me.

Saturday morning, December 19, I was thinking, "What am I going to do now?" when I heard the officers downstairs talking about "a good movie tonight at the Bragman." And I heard another say he was going to the Scorpion to dance; and yet another said he was going to go dancing at Pozo Azul. I began to think of a new way to escape. From that time, with the Gillette, I began cutting the skin beneath my toes and collecting the blood in a small plastic bag I had in my cell. Also into the bag I would add my spit to increase the volume of the solution. By the end of the day I had a big collection of that material.

From the window that evening, I watched and counted as each of the officers left the jail to go to the movie and to the dances. Finally, I calculated only one to be left in the building to guard the prisoners. Then at about eight o'clock I heard footsteps coming up the stairs. It was a Sandinista guard named Bob who answered when I called out, "Give me some water, please. I need some water." When Bob opened the door to my cell he saw me looking very sick with blood (from the plastic bag) pouring from my mouth. Quickly, he went to the kitchen and returned with a glass of ice water. I said, "My head is feeling hot. Please take me into the yard so that I can put cold water onto myself. I feel like I am dying." Bob said "O.K. Come."

As I walked down the stairs with Bob's M16 pointed at me from about five feet away, I said to my God, "If this is your will, then help me, please, to do it right."

As we came walking down the staircase, which was on the outside on the building, we passed by the window of a cell that held Uriel Zuniga, the Miskito leader and friend who had been involved in the altercation at the Prinzapolca church. Uriel had been imprisoned two months longer than I. When I passed by his window, I said softly, "I'm going. Let's go." Uriel grunted, indicating he was not willing to try to escape with me. I looked into the window as I passed and saw my friend lying on the bed looking swollen and full of sickness.

Into the yard we walked, with Bob following about five or six feet behind and a little to the side of me. I bent over the barrel, which was full of rainwater, and began dousing my head and making noises like I was heaving and gagging. From the corner of my eye I could see the guard move toward me. Then he dropped the gun barrel to the ground as he looked for evidence of my vomiting. He said, "You're not vomiting anything. You're not vomiting shit!" I replied, "Yes, I vomit shit," as I spun around quickly giving him a hard chop in the throat. As he was falling backward I grabbed the M16, then pounded his skull with the butt end several times until he was lying quiet and still. Then I took that same part of the gun and jammed it hard into his chest two times before reaching beneath his belt to get the Soviet Makarov pistol that was tucked inside. I left him for dead.*

Just then I heard footsteps coming from inside of the jail. It sounded like three or maybe four people, so I ran behind the building toward the bluff that fronted the sea and dove into the air with a weapon in each hand. The drop was about twenty-

---

*Five years later, Ráfaga realized that he had not killed the guard, when he found himself at the peace table sitting directly across from Bob. The escape was never discussed.

five feet down to the beach. I landed in a mud hole, surrounded by a big clump of bush. Covered with mud, I could hardly run or even walk fast. I went into the sea to let the waves clean the mud from my body. While I was cleaning myself and the guns, four or five automatic weapons from the bluff above began firing into the bush below. Maybe five hundred or six hundred rounds were spent, and as the bullets would strike the trees the sparks would fly.

I had decided ahead of time in which direction I would run. To the south were the pier and many Sandinista houses and offices; to the north were Miskito neighborhoods and the bush. The Sandinistas would expect me to run to the north; therefore, I began running southward toward the pier, about one and one-half miles away.

I ran in the water so there would be no footprints for the soldiers to follow. As I was running, four or five men with automatic weapons began firing their guns from the beach below the bluff. At first they were firing toward the south, and they even traveled in my direction for a few minutes. But soon they turned back to the north and began traveling in that direction, spraying the bush and beach with a storm of bullets as they ran, unable to locate me in the darkness.

When I was about a half a mile from the pier, I dove into the water with the M16 strapped to my back and the pistol in my hand. My mother's house was near the sea where I had begun to swim, and when I looked back in that direction, I could see much activity. The house was surrounded by all kinds of vehicles. I could hear loud voices and I could see flashlight beams darting through the darkness.

The weather was strong, so the sea was rough. Large waves engulfed me time and time again as I swam toward that part of the pier that was not lighted. Once underneath the structure, I climbed up into the pilings, then positioned myself a few feet beneath the floor. In that position I remained for about four hours or more. There was much activity on the pier. Sandinista soldiers were ordering the Miskitos out of their catboats, which were making ready to sail. I heard the soldiers say, "No one is leaving until we find Reynaldo Reyes!" I could hear conversations all around. Two voices I recognized were those of my uncles Victor and Pancho, saying, "Tonight the Sandinistas are going to kill our boy." Those two were crying for me, and all of the Miskitos on the pier were afraid for me.

I began counting the bullets in the M-16 and in the pistol. There were thirty rounds in the rifle and thirteen in the pistol's clip. I said to myself, "If the Sandinistas find me hiding here, I am going to kill forty-three soldiers before I die. I won't let them capture me alive."

Many vehicles were moving up and down the pier. Sandinista gunboats were shining big lights along the beaches and across the top of the water. I could hear gunshots coming from all sections of Puerto Cabezas. It sounded like a war. Above me, Miskitos were talking about how the soldiers had shut down all the businesses in town, closed the Bragman and the Scorpion and Pozo Azul, then had ordered everyone to their homes.

At about two A.M. the noise began to settle. The soldiers' guns became quiet, and it seemed as though all of the searching for Reynaldo Reyes had finished for the night, so I climbed down into the water to continue swimming. I swam about one mile south of the pier, then came out of the sea to walk into some big bush. From the bush I came to a little road, where I walked for two miles without seeing any person or car. Into the neighborhood called Barrio Beach I crept like a cat, with the M16 ready to fire. All was still and very quiet. I sensed that I should go to the house of an old woman named Luisa. She was a fanatic Moravian, very respected in the area. I crept to the door of Luisa's house and softly knocked. Immediately the door opened wide and she said, "Come inside. I have bathwater ready and food for you. I have been ready and waiting to receive you. There will be no problem for you to stay here, Reynaldo. Last night the angels told me that you would escape and come here. That is why I prepared everything for you. Don't worry. The Sandinistas will never capture you again."

I stayed hidden in Luisa's house December 20, 21, and part of the next day. On the morning of December 22, before it was daylight, a group of Miskito men came to the house to take me to another house about two blocks away. In that house there lived a Jamaican man whose name I cannot recall, but the people who were helping me complete my escape trusted him because he was married to a Miskito woman from the village of Wawa. Every Miskito in the neighborhood knew that I was there, and all of them behaved like watchmen or bodyguards. While I was in that house, a message reporting my whereabouts and well-being was taken to my mother, and arrangements for transporting her to Awastara were explained. The Miskito people had made a plan to take me first to Wawa and then a few days later to Awastara.

At about ten o'clock on the night of December 22, two men, Erwin How (whom we called Chino) and Nicolás Niubal, came to the Jamaican's house with a car to take me to a village called Lamlaya, from where I was to take a boat up the river to Wawa. I told Chino and Nicolás that if the Sandinistas stopped the car, they were to say that I was forcing them at gunpoint to drive me to Lamlaya. I did not want to be captured again. I wanted to fight or die. But Nicolás said, "Give me your pistol. If the Sandinistas come, I am going to die fighting with you."

We saw not one soldier along that three-mile road to Lamlaya. When we arrived, a boat was waiting with its motor running. I walked directly to the boat from the car, and just as we were leaving the shore to motor up the Río Karata (Wawa), a big truck full of Sandinista soldiers came into view. Quickly we sped away from Lamlaya and continued for an hour and twenty minutes running full speed all the way up the Karata to Wawa.

As the boat pulled into Wawa, I saw hundreds of pine torches waving to me along the bank. The whole Wawa community, about fifteen hundred people, were singing and saluting me with "Yamni balram Wawa ra [Welcome to Wawa]." A Sumo Indian named Milton, the Moravian minister in Wawa, greeted me as I stepped out of the boat. He said that everyone had been gathered since seven P.M. praying for my safe arrival. Milton and I walked to the church as the citizens followed behind. There in the Moravian church in the early morning hours, the people made prayers of thanks to God for my safe arrival.

In that village I remained four days before going on to Awastara. During those four days, I trained with a group of fifty to sixty

MISURASATA warriors who were camped there, practicing with .22-caliber rifles and with bows and arrows. Then on the night of December 26, I was put into a motorboat to make the trip to Awastara.

Down the river to the ocean we cut through the darkness, then went far out to sea before turning back to the north, so that when we passed Puerto Cabezas we would be far from the sight of any Sandinistas. At six A.M. we landed on the beach one mile from Awastara.

About ten Awastara men were waiting at the seashore for me. One of the men was Jerry Morales, the Moravian minister in Awastara. He greeted me, then we walked a mile to the church, where there was a service of praise and thanksgiving. It was in the church that I first saw my mother since having escaped from the jail in Puerto Cabezas. Many people had come from other villages to welcome me. The church was full and the people spilled out into the yard. After the service I stayed in the churchyard visiting with my Indian brothers from Dakura and Pahara as well as those from my home village of Awastara. All were happy and crying for joy because I was alive and with them in that moment.

The Wawa people had given me three hundred bullets. I was preparing to fight, so I gathered twelve Awastara boys who had hunting rifles to begin training with me. Having made my decision, I sent for two of my children, who were with my friend, Emma Muller, in Puerto Cabezas. (The other children were in Chontales with their mother at the time.)

Emma had twice before come to Awastara to bring me clothes, medicine, and other things I needed. And it was Emma who brought Lester and Magdaly to my mother's house in Awastara. I had been staying in the bush with my twelve boys; it was too dangerous to be around my mother's house, because Sandinistas passed by often. When Emma brought the children, she came in the night so no one would know they were there.

I stayed with my two babies in that house for four days loving them, playing with them, and finally explaining to them why I must leave them to fight against the Sandinistas. I said to them,

"I am going to war, going to fight, and maybe I am going to Honduras. But if I don't die—if they don't kill me—I will return. I have big hopes of returning to live with you." Magdaly said, "Papa, why are you going to fight?" I replied, "Because I believe it is my obligation to fight with my brothers for our Indian rights." She was crying and saying, "How are we going to live without you? We love you too much. We cannot live without you." I told her, "Yes, Daly, you will live, and so will many other Indian babies, because the fathers have gone to the war to fight for your lives." Lastly, I told my only son, "Lester, if I die in the war, someday you are going to take my place and try to continue fighting for Indian rights. Do not cry for me if they kill me, because I want to fight for our sacred principles or die, if that is God's will." I said good-bye to my babies, then returned to my boys in the bush, where we stayed through the month of January 1982 preparing ourselves to fight. It would be four years before I would see Lester and Magdaly again.

Two days after the children had been taken back to Puerto Cabezas, a Sandinista officer named Dale Daniels, along with a few soldiers, came to my mother's house demanding to know my whereabouts. When my sister Sidonia said, "We don't know where he is," the officer began hitting her with his fist, knocking her to the floor. The soldiers begged their leader to stop beating her. Then they threw everything that was in the house out into the yard—furniture, clothes, books. They then ripped, slashed, and shot full of holes every single thing that was in the yard. From the bush I was watching as this bad thing happened to my family. I was ready, now, to fight with great anger and a vengeance growing inside me.

The Sandinistas began pulling the Indians out of their homes along the Río Coco in 1981 and 1982. The government stated that their reason for doing this was to "protect" the Indians from the fighting between the Sandinista and Contra forces along the Honduran border, where the Río Coco flows.* But

---

*Around this time the propaganda war began to escalate, with the U.S. government accusing Sandinistas of crossing Río Coco to massacre Miskito refugees.

this reason was not valid. My people were not "protected." They were murdered.

The soldiers mistreated the Indian people as they were forced to move from their river villages to faraway *asientamientos* (resettlement communities). The Indians sacrificed much, and they themselves were sacrificed. It was not "protection" but persecution that the Sandinistas forced upon my people. As the Indians were forced out of their homes, leaving all their possessions, the Sandinistas burned all the buildings in the little villages and destroyed all the crops and livestock.

Made to walk from their villages along the rivers to the *asientamientos*, many of my people died. Some died of natural causes brought about by the hard journey, while others died at the violent hands of the Sandinista army. The Indians in transit were not provided with food or water, nor were their medical and health needs attended to. Many were also injured owing to the difficulty of the walk and to the violence brought on them by the government troops who were managing the transfers.

Many couples became separated from each other and from their children. Some families tried to escape to Honduras so they would not be forced to go to the relocation camps. Other families tried to escape from the soldiers during the transfer, becoming separated in the ordeal. In some cases, the mother would get away from the soldiers and the father would not. The man would have to stay in Nicaragua and the woman would have to find her way to Honduras.

Usually Miskito people travel in little canoes called *pitban* or *batu*, but the Sandinista troops forced the people to walk. Some of the very old or very sick people could not keep up with the pace set by the soldiers. The Sandinistas shot the old and sick ones and just left them by the roadside to die. Some of my Indian sisters who gave birth during the journey were forced by the soldiers to abandon their little babies on the road. If the mother protested or tried to remain behind to care for the newborn, then both the mother and baby were executed by the government soldiers. Probably between one thousand and fifteen hundred Miskito were killed.

This is a macabre story that I am sharing with you. It makes my heart cry. I do not want to go any deeper into those events. That is all I can say. This is the truth of what happened to our people during that time. Since the ancient days, this sort of tragedy had never before happened to the Miskito nation. Not since the Spaniards came into this region four or five hundred years ago have we seen this kind of tragedy. Neither have other governments to which we have been subjected ever treated us in this barbaric way.

The Sandinistas showed us brutality that had not been seen in Central America for five hundred years. They forced the Miskito people out of their homes so we would not give refuge to the Indian revolutionaries who were fighting along the Nicaraguan-Honduran border. They killed, mutilated, and tortured our people simply because they believed each one of us to be their enemy. But that was not true.

For the past two years the Sandinista government has been apologizing to us and to the world for what was allowed to happen to our people during the relocations of the early 1980s. I believe that the government is sincere in its appeal, to some measure. But it is difficult to forgive the behavior of the Sandinistas, though the apology is certainly in order and welcomed. It will take much time and effort on both sides for the Sandinistas and the Miskitos to build trust and confidence in each other. And even if relations are good again at some time in the future, there will be eternal scars marking the spiritual and psychological wounds inflicted on our Miskito nation by the persecution.

The news of what the Sandinista government was doing to our Indian brothers and sisters on the Río Coco reached me and my twelve boys while we were in the bush between Awastara and Sandy Bay in January 1982. At the same time, many Indian leaders had come into Nicaragua with their revolutionaries from the training camps in Honduras. In the bush outside Sandy Bay, I met Comandante Sutum, who invited me and my twelve boys to join with him and his thirty-three Miskito warriors to fight against the Sandinista in Sandy Bay. Three other co-mandantes were with Sutum at that time: a man named Rufus from Kum, on the Río Coco; another by the name of Yanki; and a comandante called Shang. We all joined together to make a revolution in Sandy Bay. Including myself, we num-bered forty-nine, and Comandante Sutum was our leader. Only twelve of us had good weapons. I had the M16, but most of the boys had only .22-caliber long rifles and 20-gauge shot-guns—the old kind used for killing deer and game.

I started to fight against the Sandinista soldiers at Sandy Bay on January 29, 1982. We fought for three continuous hours, until night closed in on us. On January 30, when morning came, I backed off a mile and a half from my position because Comandante Shang had been wounded. I carried him away from the area to what I believed was a safer place. But the Sandinistas were waiting, and there we fought again, that time for forty-five minutes. I never saw who or how many Sandinistas we killed during those first two battles. Since that time, I have been told by Sandy Bay civilians that plenty of Sandinistas perished in the revolution we brought there at the end of January 1982.

I sent the wounded Comandante Shang to my home village of Awastara, where he was treated and cared for until he was strong enough for the trip back to Honduras. After two weeks I arranged for him to be taken by sea to Twibila, a Miskito military base in Honduras just a few miles north of the border.

Shortly thereafter, while I camped with Timson Mateo and Bayardo Suarez on the shore of Lake Awastara, we saw a government speedboat carrying six soldiers coming across the lake to our side. We waited until they reached the shore and watched as they disrobed for a swim. I told the boys I had an idea how we might use this situation to our political advantage. We took up strategic positions in the bush around the area where three of the unsuspecting soldiers were sunning them-selves on a log while the others swam. At the given signal, the three of us fired, and all were dead in a moment. We took their official identification papers, weapons, and uniforms, then transported the bodies in their boat to the opposite shore, where we buried them. After returning to our camp, we removed the motor from the boat and handed it over to a group of MISURA soldiers camped near Awastara. I took the official papers and composed a letter in Spanish (pretending to be one of the Sandinistas) to the Sandinista government stating that we six Sandinista soldiers were opposed to the aggression against the Miskitos and were hereby giving notice of our desertion to Honduras in order to join with the counterrevolutionary forces there.

We spent the next few weeks carrying out ambushes and raids against the Sandinistas in the region north of Puerto Cabezas. For example, we knew that the people of Krukira had been terrorized three times by truckloads of Sandinistas, who came from their base at Puerto Cabezas, for the sole purpose of raping our young Miskito women in that village. The men in the village had no weapons and no way to fend off these humiliating attacks. We were asked by the old heads of the village whether we could do something about this, so after having been notified that a truckload of twenty-five to thirty Sandinistas was on its way, we took up position at a spot where the truck was likely to stop in Krukira. As the truck was stopping and the soldiers were beginning to get out, we opened fire on the gasoline tank. There was a big explosion. Some of the soldiers were killed, and others ran into the bush and traveled on foot back to Puerto Cabezas. That put an end to the use of Krukira as a recreation area, and following the incident, my gang became known as "Gasoline." We continued to engage in similar raids and ambushes on Sandinista troops in the villages of Dakura, Pahara, and Tuara.

In February I began to plan to go to Honduras. My mother, who was living in Awastara, gave me her little catboat *Pancasan* with sails and outboard motor. I put my twelve boys and myself into the little boat to make the journey to Honduras. Cordero Joseph from Awastara went as captain, and we sailed north up the Atlantic Coast and over to a little group of islands called the Miskito Keys. From there we sailed northwest right across to Honduras and went to the MISURA base at Twibila.

The next day Steadman Fagoth and a group of Honduran military leaders flew by helicopter from a MISURA base in the Honduran village of RusRus to the base at Twibila. Fagoth and the Honduran leaders Major Elec Sanchez, Captain Luki, and a lieutenant, came to Twibila to speak with me about the war being fought between the Sandinistas and MISURA in Nicaragua. We spent a full day talking about the battles and the situation on the Nicaraguan Atlantic Coast. Then Fagoth and the three Honduran leaders flew back to RusRus. The following day the four of them returned to Twibila for more talks with me. On that day they asked me many questions about how Gasoline, under my leadership, had had such success. They also asked me about my ideas and plans for the future.

My boys had spoken to Fagoth the previous day about how I was a good leader. The boys had spoken well of me and of how I fought those battles. Comandantes Yanki, Shang, and Sutum also had spoken to Fagoth about their good experiences with me in Nicaragua.

You see, it had been Fagoth's way to place inexperienced comandantes in charge of the Miskito boys fighting against the revolution. Many of the boys were young, inexperienced, and scared. Also, some of the comandantes were incompetent to lead the troops, and this combination had produced some regrettable situations—like the one that nearly occurred in the fighting at Sandy Bay in January, when Comandante Shang had been shot by the Sandinista soldiers. Shang's boys had become frightened and had run away, leaving their leader to die or be captured. Fagoth said that had it not been for the actions of Reynaldo Reyes and his boys, Comandante Shang would have perished. The boys made up a song of praise for me about that situation when Comandante Shang was wounded in Sandy Bay and rescued by us.

Ráfaga Layan Kupia
By Esteban (Chingo Lingo) Morze*
Iralaya, Honduras, 1982
(In Miskito)

Siakua kati 29, 1982 Yuwa
1:00 A.M. Aimaki Kan
Komandante Ráfaga; pat, pat
Tawi kaiki kan aituk tika nanira
Bara naku wikata:

Tuktan sibri para, Dawan yawon wal so
Dawan wan ta brisa, witin ba yawan pailat kasa.
Pain alki bas raks kam nani ba.
Tisku, tisku piuwara lawana sat sat walma
RPG-7 binka walma, mayugue binka walma
M60 binka walma, baku sin mortero bink walma.

Binka sat, sat, walma sakuna lukan ka lika
Kumi sa ¡Tagusgalpa pri apia kaka pruwaya!
Komandante Ráfaga kupia karnira layan kupia

Limi siksa kupia, yakal wahinka kupia.
Siksak ra arrastre ra auyasa.
Alai limi baku, layan baku kuasi, kuasi
Dimi auya kupia bila karnira
¡Fuegoo dimi wap diara ba yas!
¡Tagusgalpa pri apia kaka pruwaya!

Ráfaga, Courageous as the Lion

The twenty-ninth of January 1982
At one in the morning,
Comandante Ráfaga is restless.
He stops and tells the warriors:

---

*Esteban (Chingo Lingo) Morze fell in combat at Bom-Sirpe at the age of 24 in October 1985. He was the father of three children. Ráfaga remembers him as "one of the best guitarists ever produced by the Miskito people. He was also a composer and singer in Honduras who was offered many lucrative contracts by nationally famous groups, but he always refused them because it was his delight to sing to his people for free."

Don't worry, boys. God is with us.
God is guiding us. He is our pilot.
Hold your weapons firmly.
Soon, very soon, we will hear different songs.
The RPG-7s, *mayuguez*, M60s, mortars, FALs,
    and AK-45s will sing.

We will hear different melodies,
but we have only one aim:
A free Atlantic Coast or death!
My valiant comandante crouches and advances
Like a lion, like a black panther,

And then he hears the command, Fire!
A free Atlantic Coast or death !
Advance, advance boys, the victory is ours!

My boys told Fagoth how I was well prepared and self-trained to fight the battles. They told him how through my ideas and plans I had never led them into any situation to be hurt or lost.

Fagoth knew perfectly well that I had been a guerrilla in the West against Somoza and later was in the Ejercito Popular Sandinista. The Indian counterrevolutionaries were impressed by my astute decisions and courageous acts in the most hellish moments in the heat of battle. When you have an enemy in front of you who is often much better equipped with sophisticated weapons and backed by the air force, navy, and infantry, fighting with elevated morale for having expelled the tyrant Somoza at gunpoint, you face a fierce challenge. We encountered these fellows three or four times a day and were continuously pursued by their air force.

Another thing that moved my boys was my comprehension, execution, discipline, and sharing of scientific knowledge, counsel, and instantaneous inventions on the battlefield. Let me describe each of these a bit more.

Comprehension. I have said that Sutum was my comandante. I knew that Comandante Sutum was extremely courageous, with much love for his people and his combatants and with a great sense that it was possible to exterminate those *piricuaco* (bungling) Sandinistas, as he called them, yet I knew that he had zero experience as a guerrilla. But when they told me that he was my comandante I accepted and comprehended. I had much more experience than he, but submitted willingly to the authority of the organization.

Execution. My motto was "He who hits first, hits twice"; that is, always count on the time factor in our favor, not to be surprised by the enemy, not to be ambushed by the enemy. I used to tell the boys, "It is clear that there is no such thing as a small enemy—we are fighting for a just cause, we want to see the liberation of our people, and we want to live to see that day. Our war is a holy war." Our primary strength was our allegiance to our Divine Commander, Jehovah God of the armies. Before and after our battles we raised our pledges to heaven. Our actions were planned by me and then replanned with my subalterns. I asked questions of my boys to make sure we all knew whatever valuable details anyone knew about the terrain and the upcoming battle plans. Sometimes seemingly insignificant details would become very important in a deeper analysis of our situation. I really believe that Divine Providence gave me the gift of leadership and charisma. Because of this my boys always accepted my orders 100 percent.

Discipline. My mottoes here were "The law begins in the home" and the lesson that I learned from my maternal grandfather Jefinaias Davis, who now is a hundred years old, who said, "Without sufficient moral authority in yourself, don't ask for morality from others." From this and other lessons I learned to try to be an example for the boys both on and off the battlefield. One of my main worries therefore was discipline for each "disciple-soldier." The rules were to demonstrate your discipline through love and respect for the civilian population and to respect the physical integrity of a captured enemy. Your respect and discipline are things that the prisoner will understand. Torture, both physical and psychological, creates hate and commitment. Your prisoner should learn why we are fighting. We told the prisoners: "We are fighting for the reclamation of indigenous rights trampled by governments and leaders. We are fighting against communism and not against the Communist. We hate communism, not the Communist. This fratricidal and genocidal war will end if you stop fighting." In this way I convinced many prisoners to fight with us. Other comandantes thought I was just being kind to my ex-comrades—they often killed their prisoners of war.

Sharing knowledge. Before receiving aid from Reagan and the CIA, the Miskito counterrevolutionaries did not have weapons for war, just hunting rifles and .22s. Most of them had bows and arrows that we made ourselves. After December 1981, when I arrived in Awastara, I began to teach what I had learned through my long years in the guerrilla war with my ex-comrade Sandinistas. I taught them how to deactivate mines and how to use them. I taught them how to make Molotov cocktails (something I had learned in Cuba), how to bomb bridges, and how to use automatic weapons, rifles, and support weapons when we captured some. In January 1982, in one of our ambushes, we captured a communications radio that was of great use to us. We were able to monitor and capture the coded messages of our enemies, and the enemy unconsciously helped us in our actions against them. I had a knack for communications technology that I discovered when I had been with the Sandinistas. Two of my young Indians learned this technology very quickly, so we knew most of the movements of the Sandinista troops, which allowed us to ambush them frequently. I did not need to teach them to read maps and compasses, because they were already the masters and lords of the whole Atlantic Coast. They knew it from north to south and west to east. They knew how to cross a river with thirty to forty pounds on their shoulders and their weapons in their hands. My personal tactic was to use long ropes to cross rivers. But the Indians are real champions in swimming, like fish in water. They did not need a rope to cross lakes and rivers. Any modern tactician would be amazed by Indian skills in our mountains and waters. When I started to talk to them about how to creep forward on their bellies, an Indian, Bayardo Suarez, said, "We already know how to do that. You're trying to say we should move like a lizard or iguana!"

For these gifts I was respected by my people and especially by the Miskito warriors under my command. When they saw me fight with such skill in those first battles, they considered me their comandante. Thus I gained their confidence without really seeking it. I always tried to be democratic, but each knew that a superior order could not be discussed, it had to be carried out.

Fagoth and the Honduran military leaders had no choice but to recognize that I was already acting as comandante. They put me in charge of 460 Miskito warriors based at Twibila in Honduras.

The War Name "Ráfaga": A Gift from the Boys

The boys did not have good weapons, and the M16 I had used in January 1982 at Sandy Bay had been ruined. When the M16 is fired too much it gets hot and jams.

At Twibila in February, I received only one .22-caliber rifle to use because Steadman Fagoth was not able to provide us with the automatic weapons we needed at that time.

As Comandante Reynaldo Reyes, I led twenty-five boys out of Honduras on a mission to Nicaragua. On our way into Kum, where it had been reported that a group of Sandinista soldiers were encamped, we were surrounded by a heavy force of fifty or more Sandinistas with real automatic weapons.

The Sandinistas trapped six of us where we could not get out. My boys used all of their bullets. I had eighteen bullets in my rifle—all it could hold—and eighteen more in my belt. Eleven soldiers charged us, and I was pushed to open fire at close range. My only thoughts were to save my boys and to kill those Sandinistas who were pressing on us.

I began firing that .22-caliber long hunting rifle like it was a machine gun. I had to do that to save my boys because the Sandinistas were going to kill us. I was firing fast—shooting so fast—*Rapido! Rapido! Rapido!* When it was over, there were eleven soldiers dead right in front of us and I had not used the last of the eighteen bullets in my rifle.

Then my boys, instead of calling me "hero," called me "Rá-faga," which is a Spanish word that means a burst or volley of fire, or a gust of strong wind. You see, I was shooting so fast

67

with that .22 that it looked like I had an automatic weapon. That is how my boys gave me my *nombre de guerra*, Ráfaga.

So, you see, the name comes from a brave deed, and I will always feel proud about how my boys gave me my war name. That is exactly how, on February 16, 1982, the Ráfaga name began.

You may wonder how it feels to take the life of another human. How did I feel? Now I am going to give you that answer.

From the time of my growing up until my young days of traveling all around, I had never fought with any man—never made trouble with anybody. Some men take a few drinks, start to feel brave, and fight or beat up another man and make trouble. Well, I have never been a troublemaker. I never had fought anybody. I would never just pick up a gun and see a man and *bam, bam,* shoot him like that. I am not a man who beats his wife or his woman. All of those violent things I never did. I never liked it and I never did it. I never had an enemy. Everybody had always loved me and cared for me.

But when I was in the war, I had to fight. I had to kill to stay alive. If I had not killed those enemies, they would have killed me and my boys.

As a leader, I saw my boys get shot. When my boys got shot, I would often take them up into my arms and hold them as the life left their bodies.

When I saw my boys dying like that, I had the feeling, Well, fight more and kill all of the enemy off! See if I could finish all of them off! When I started to think in that way, I felt angry and I got mad. And that is how I was feeling when I killed those eleven government soldiers at close range in Kum on February 16, 1982.

Now I do not feel sad or mad. I do not feel anything, because I try to forget that which has passed already. I do not want to keep it in mind to dwell on or anything of that sort. In fact, I want to apologize to the readers of my life story for having to use the word *kill*. But all this happened to me, and I had to fight like that to save my life and to protect my boys. When you are in a war, you have to fight that way. I believe maybe that wars start from above. I see it in the Bible how there has always been warring—King David and others. Jehovah God used to give directions for wars. There was war in heaven between the angel Lucifer and the angel Michael. Perhaps that is the reason why we men have kept on fighting since the ancient days up until now.

I used to think about war and the reason for war. My boys and I would discuss those ideas. Perhaps this warring is not willed by us but is the Lord's will. Maybe, with the Lord's will, it happens that way. That is the reason why before every mission, before every battle, I made a prayer to my God. I always said a prayer for me and for my boys.

That place called Twibila in Honduras where we had our base was not a village before Fagoth made a base there. No one ever lived there before. It was at Twibila that I was put in charge of the 460 Miskito warriors who were camped there.

Three miles south of Twiliba, just across the border, is a village called Cabo Gracias a Dios. The name means Cape Thanks to God, but we Miskito call it Old Cape (Sita Awala). When Christopher Columbus made his fourth voyage to the New World, he came to what is now Central America and the first little village that he found was this place Cabo Gracias a Dios. When Columbus arrived at that village, only Miskito Indians lived there. We the Indians respect Old Cape and love it.

Early in 1982 the Sandinista government removed all the Indians living in Old Cape to a place called Sumobila and to Puerto Cabezas. Left behind at Old Cape were many milk cows, pigs, and horses. After the Indians had been marched away from Old Cape, the soldiers burned all of the houses; the Moravian, Catholic, and Church of God churches; the schools; and other buildings in our old Indian village.

Sometimes my boys and I would visit Old Cape from our base at Twibila. Later the Sandinista soldiers began returning to Old Cape to eat the cows and pigs that had been left there by our people. There had been occasions before when we saw Sandinistas strolling about Old Cape, but we never considered fighting against them. Those soldiers just came and walked about and looked around. But when they came to butcher the animals, I started to prepare my boys to attack.

On February 25, 1982, twenty-two of my boys from Twibila and I surrounded the soldiers at Cabo Gracias a Dios. There appeared to be about sixty Sandinistas. We fired the first shots and fought very hard for fifty or sixty minutes. I counted thirteen dead Sandinistas. Afterward, we returned to our Twibila base. On February 26 and 27 we came again to Old Cape and gave the Sandinistas another hot fight.

On March 1, two days after we finished the fight at Cabo Gracias, we went over to Bihmuna, less than twenty miles from Old Cape. I took 210 Miskito boys from Twibila. Also along with us were the comandantes Rufus and Sutum. There were no Miskitos living in Bihmuna at that time because, like those at Old Cape, they had been moved out by government troops to *asientamientos*. In Bihmuna the Sandinistas had converted the schoolhouse into a command headquarters, and many soldiers were living there. Others were living in two other barracks in the community. Because I knew there were no civilians in Bihmuna, only Sandinistas, I went over and fought them.

At four o'clock in the morning we went in and bombed the schoolhouse down. We threw a grenade into the command post. Then we launched an RPG-7 rocket in there, too. Quite a few Sandinista people who were sleeping inside that old schoolhouse got killed. I believe there may have been as many as fifty to sixty men inside when we bombed them.

Not all of the Sandinistas in Bihmuna were killed. Some were outside guarding the area, and others were sleeping in other buildings. Also, there were two smaller barracks in the community where soldiers were stationed. But the ones who were asleep in the old schoolhouse surely died.

For that mission in Bihmuna, I had three or four boys stay close to me to work as messengers transmitting orders. At five o'clock in the morning, one hour into the battle, one of my messenger boys was shot dead. His name was Jaime Salomon. He was seventeen. Four or five minutes later, another messenger, by the name of Howard, who was twenty, was wounded. Not long after that, another of my trusted boys, Pablo, whom we called Flat Nose, was killed when his own gun backfired.

He was twenty-five. Between five o'clock and five-thirty in the morning, three of my boys were shot—two dead and one wounded. Pablo and Jaime were dead. Jaime was from Sandy Bay, and Pablo's home was Puerto Cabezas.

At six o'clock in the morning one of the barracks caught fire and burned. We kept on fighting. Next, another barracks caught fire and burned. We kept fighting. Then we launched a bomb at the guard tower, taking it down also. In the midst of the battle Comandante Rufus, who was my second in command, ran away. Afterward, I put Comandante Sutum as my second. He took the boys to the other side from where I was positioned. At eleven o'clock in the morning another boy, the one we called Mateo, was killed. We kept on fighting.

Out of sixty or more Sandinistas fighting in Bihmuna that day, only about nine survived the initial attack. Those nine were hiding in a trench, and from that protected position they kept on fighting hard. I could not get in close to them because there was a clearing—no trees, bush, or tall grasses—between me and the trench, and that made it dangerous to get in there. Comandante Sutum and six boys ran across that open field charging the trench. The government soldiers killed three of the boys as they ran. When those three fell, four more of Sutum's boys ran up to take the places of their dead brothers. Then all eight including Sutum dove into that trench firing their weapons.

Sutum was shot three times in the leg, but kept on fighting. The trench was long, and Sutum had to keep on fighting a long time in order to finish off the four or five Sandinistas there.

The government soldiers never got any reinforcements because we had burned down the radio command post at the very beginning of the attack.

The three Miskito boys who were killed while storming the trench were all Sandy Bay boys: Joaquín Barquero, Tekere, and Ramos. In all, seven Miskito boys were killed in that battle at Bihmuna, which lasted from four o'clock in the morning until five o'clock in the afternoon—we fought for thirteen continuous hours.

My heart cries when I remember Jaime and the others who died that day. Yes, I loved my boys. But what to do? What is past is past.

It was during the big fight at Bihmuna that I was wounded for the first time. A Sandinista bullet passed my head and grazed my right shoulder. If I had not rolled in the right direction, I would be a dead man now.

Three or four shots came at me. I could not tell where they were coming from. I saw one coconut tree close by and prayed to my God that I would be able to make it to safety behind that tree. I did get behind that tree, when suddenly one of the Sandinista bullets hit the trunk and exploded powder into my eyes. My shoulder was bleeding and my eyes were burning. I was looking all about for the Sandinistas but could not catch sight of them. Then I rolled over flat on my back and kept very still because I was hurting.

While I was in that position staring up into the treetops, I saw the soldier who had been firing at me. He was high up in the top of a big mango tree. I suppose he must have thought he had killed me, because after I had rolled onto my back, he quit firing at me and was looking for another target.

My right hand was made useless from the shoulder wound, so I knew that I could not handle a gun with that hand. The weapon lying by my left side was a carbine. I had in my sight the Sandinista high up in the tree when I quickly grabbed the carbine with my left hand, rolled over onto my right side, and fired into the branches. That Sandinista fell right out of that tree. I walked over to where he was lying on the ground and found him dead with a big hole in his side.

It was about one o'clock in the afternoon. I kept on fighting even though my shoulder was still hurting. Another soldier began shooting hard at me. That one really wanted to kill me. He would not quit firing for even one minute. It is my idea that he must have thought that I was a paid mercenary from another country because I was not dressed like the other Indian fighters. I was wearing a blue cap, and a long blue jacket, and blue pants. Also, I had on dark sunglasses. My boys were dressed in camouflage clothes.

The Sandinista was mad and he was after me. He kept shooting at me more and more until he finally shot and broke the carbine out of my left hand. There on the ground nearby was another carbine, the one Rufus had left behind, so I took it up into my right hand, which by now had some feeling sensation and in my left hand I held a 9-millimeter pistol. I was firing both weapons at that persistent Sandinista when I got shot again—this time in the leg. I could feel my warm blood running down my leg and my whole body on that side got numb. I could not move. I said to myself, "Well, I really got shot this time. That is my warm blood I feel. Hot! Burning all over where he shot me."

I never did look at that wound. I was just creeping, creeping on my belly and dragging my dead leg behind me, trying to get to this one big tree. When I finally got there, I looked at my wound, but I could not see any blood. Then I saw the bullet hole in my canteen and realized that the "warm blood" running down my leg was, in truth, only warm water spilling from the bullet hole in my canteen. I began laughing out loud at myself behind that big tree for believing that I had been mortally wounded by a can of water!

In December 1983, thousands of Miskito families walked from Francia Sirpe, Nicaragua, to Honduras. Ráfaga was a leader of the relocation, named Mission Alpha Uno. Photograph by Lee Shapiro (reprinted by permission).

Along the Miskito trek from Francia Sirpe, Nicaragua, to Honduras, December 1983. Photograph by Lee Shapiro (reprinted by permission).

Salvador Schlaefer, Catholic bishop of Northern Zelaya, Nicaragua (second from left), and Father Wendelin Shafer (third from right) accompanied the Miskitos on their December 1983 trek to Honduras. Ráfaga credits the success of the journey, which he helped to lead, to the presence of these two religious figures. The names of the other individuals are not known. 1985. Photograph by Lee Shapiro (reprinted by permission).

Above: Miskito guerrillas patrol the Río Coco, which divides Honduras and Nicaragua. Photograph by Lee Shapiro (reprinted by permission). *Below:* Dialogue at Yulo, May 17, 1986. Left to right: Hazel Law, Tomás Borge, Ráfaga, Barbon. Photographer unknown; photo courtesy of Ráfaga.

Ráfaga with Native American movement leader Bill Means, Yulo, 1987. Photographer unknown; photo courtesy of Ráfaga.

Above: Comandantes Barbon (far left), Juan Salgado (center), Sutum (left of Ráfaga, far right) gathered near Wawabar for dialogue with Sandinistas, 1987. Photographer unknown, photo courtesy of Ráfaga. *Below:* Citizens of Puerto Cabezas welcoming a Cuban ship bringing medicine, coffee, and flour. Puerto Cabezas, March 1987.

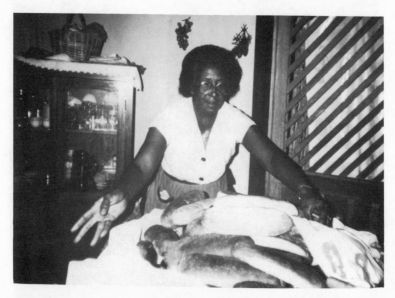

Above: Carolyn Bush, baker, proud of the fruit of her day's work.
Puerto Cabezas, March 1987. Photograph by J. K. Wilson. *Below:*
Ráfaga working with U.S. construction brigade on foundation of new
market, Puerto Cabezas, March 1987. Photograph by J. K. Wilson.

Above: Ráfaga welcoming repatriated Miskito on pier. Puerto Cabezas, 1987. Photograph by J. K. Wilson. *Below:* Miskito house made of pine and palm, stilts providing ventilation. Lamlaya, April 1987. Photograph by J. K. Wilson.

Miskito catboat leaving Puerto Cabezas pier for Río Coco, April 1987.
Photograph by J. K. Wilson.

Above: Dialogue of KISAN por la Paz with Sandinistas at Wawaboom, 1987. Banner reads, "For peace and autonomy, we coastal people will continue to struggle." Photograph by Ráfaga. *Below:* Community of Yulo, where the dialogue for peace officially began. A Moravian church can be seen in the foreground. 1987. Photograph by Ráfaga.

Above: Left to right: Comandantes Guillermo Recta, Ráfaga, Sutum. Puerto Cabezas, 1987. Photographer unknown; photograph courtesy of J. K. Wilson. *Below:* Members of KISAN por la Paz in training for defense of the peace zones. Sukatpin, 1987. Photograph by Ráfaga.

Ráfaga's uncle Abraham Esteban Pinner, translator of the interviews, with J. K. Wilson. Managua, November 1987. Photograph by Ráfaga.

Above: Ráfaga and his children. From left to right: Mariluz, Marileen, Magdaly, Lester, Ráfaga, and Marisol. Managua, November 1987. Photograph by J. K. Wilson. *Below:* J. K. Wilson with Ráfaga's granddaughter, Miccita. Managua, November 1987. Photograph by Ráfaga.

Ráfaga in the rose garden at his Managua residence, 1988. Photographer unknown; photograph courtesy of Ráfaga.

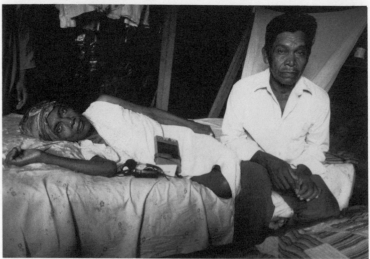

Above: Miskito war orphans at Yulo, June 1988. Photograph by Ráfaga. *Below:* Manuela Chavarria Bilis, Ráfaga's mother, with her husband, Koban Chavarria Bilis, Ráfaga's stepfather. This photograph was taken in Awastara, September 1989, just a few weeks before her death from cancer. There are no telephones on the Atlantic Coast; an audiotaped message, delivered by the photographer and played on the tape recorder shown here at Manuela's side, was Ráfaga's last communication with his mother. Photograph by Derrill Bazzy (reprinted by permission).

Ráfaga, upon completion of the manuscript of this book. Tulsa, Oklahoma, June 10, 1989. Photograph by Tod Sloan.

Seven / Matlalkahbipurakumi

Annealing of a Comandante

THE HEATING IN BATTLE

We finished that fight at Bihmuna after thirteen hours. When evening came down on us, we started to walk back to Old Cape, about fifteen miles away.

After we had gone just a short way, we came to a river. We stopped so I could check on the boys to see if they were all coming behind me. But ten boys did not come. I went back to find those boys and discovered that a small group of Sandinistas had them surrounded in a place we called Bihmuna Almuk (Old Bihmuna). When I saw the predicament the boys were in, I went back to the river to get the others so we could go fight again. But the boys were tired and hurting bad. They said they did not want to go back. The younger boys warned me, "You better not go back again because they are going to kill you!"

I told those cold-footed boys that I was tired and hurting too, like them. I had a fever and a shoulder wound. Also, the ground itch (fungus) on my feet was causing me much pain, but I said to those boys, "I cannot leave my boys to the Sandinista soldiers. I want to get them out, so I am going back. I would do the same for you."

So I walked back to Old Bihmuna, where the ten boys were trapped. I walked into the middle of the village and the Sandinistas spotted me. They turned all their weapons on me and bullets came like raindrops falling. I had to run zigzag, fall on the ground, run zigzag again, and then fall down quickly on the other side. Finally, I got behind a big tree so I could see where the bullets were coming from. I began to shoot my old carbine, and the Sandinistas returned a volley of automatic fire. While I drew their attention and their fire, the ten boys got out. Later, some of the boys from Old Bihmuna came looking for me and met up with the ten who had escaped. They all fought the Sandinistas until I got out.

I did not enjoy having to fight with those old World War II guns with which Fagoth had supplied us. He had given the good arms, sent by the United States, to the Honduran army just to impress the Honduran government, and gave the Indians those old M1's and thirty-thirties.

In contrast, the Sandinista air force was capable of mounting relentless, soulless attacks on us and on civilians as well. Their tactics were frightening but ineffective. We often laughed at their futile efforts. When they saw three or four of us on the ground, not knowing whether we were civilians or soldiers, they would fire five-hundred-pound rockets at us. The rockets came like guided arrows, spinning and making a thunderous sound. If they hit in the jungle, their force would tear down trees and rip through branches, sending smoke and fire everywhere. If they landed in water, fountains would shoot up thirty feet into the air, killing fish and birds. The war had a major impact on our fauna. The Sandinista air force would often drop bombs on likely hiding spots. We referred to this tactic in English as "blind shots." It was a horrible waste of munitions. They paid no attention to what they were bombing. They would regularly bomb fields of crops and towns where the guerrilla had been. To this day, there are little ponds near the towns where the rockets made craters. In 1984 there were even some signs that they used chemical weapons that killed trees and animals, but they apparently stopped using them due to international pressure. These attacks kept us moving, but we never had casualties from them. In fact, we often put out mannequins as decoys to attract fire, and the Sandinista air force would blast away at them in their eagerness to exterminate us. Their more effective strategy was to drop bags of marijuana in the rivers and on the villages in an attempt to undermine our alertness. This worked well because many of the combatants wanted to smoke it. A group of blacks from Bluefields fighting on the southern front really had a problem after discovering a marijuana cache. They began to fight among themselves, and apparently several were killed.

I was very tired walking that fifteen miles from Bihmuna to Old Cape. The journey was made more difficult because plenty of the boys were shot up, and I was shot up too. We walked two days without sleep.

On our way back to Honduras we had to pass through Bihmuna Lagoon, which is three miles wide. I was concerned about how we would get 250 boys across, many of them hurt and shot up. Also, we carried the dead ones with us so we could bury them at the seashore. In our two little catboats we put the bodies of our dead brothers and the boys who were shot up. All the rest of the boys swam across.

That lagoon was a place of danger because some water was shallow and some was deep. Also, there were alligators, barracuda, and sharks in the water. When I started across in one little catboat, it was about five-thirty in the afternoon. At the same time the boys began to swim across. When I reached the other side, I waited at the bank until every one of the boys had crossed. It was daybreak when the last of my boys came out of the water. They had been all night swimming that lagoon. I felt proud for the courage of my boys.

When all were safely on the other side, we started walking to the seashore to bury the bodies of our Indian brothers who had fallen in the battle at Bihmuna. On the way we found Rufus, the worthless coward! I told him that I was going to kill him, and he took off running again. I do not know why Fagoth put a man like Rufus to be a leader. What if I were like Rufus? I would have left those ten boys to the Sandinistas. That Rufus, a Wanki boy, was a bad fellow.

It was Sunday morning when we got to the seashore. After we had buried our brothers in a special place known to me for many years, the Sandinistas attacked us from the sea in what you call gunboats. This is the order I gave the boys: "Don't try to shoot and don't fire at them at all. Don't fire any gun at all until I give you the order or until you see me shooting, then you start firing at them!"

All of us got down low on the ground to hide. One of the big boats with thirty or forty soldiers came toward the shore close to us. When it got very near I lit fire to the boat and the boys began to shoot.

The boat sank, and the soldiers who were not dead by our bullets drowned in the sea. Everyone was killed. Most Spanish people do not know how to swim. That is the reason why so many of them were killed crossing rivers or at sea.

Another big boat came in toward the shore, and we gave them one hot fight. We won the battle, and then three of our older men boarded that white boat and took it up a river. At about nine in the morning a Sandinista plane dropped a bomb on the boat. The three men who were in it jumped into the water and pulled the boat into a mangrove bush. By the time the plane circled back, the boat was well hidden and the plane could not find it. They must have thought they had sunk it, because they flew away in the direction of Port and never did return. That night on the radio I heard a Sandinista say, "We sank one boat with guerrilla boys inside and everyone was killed." They did not report the casualties they had sustained, nor did they report the loss of two gunboats. They only reported that they had killed all the guerrilla boys on a boat. But that was not true. We were alive and walking to Old Cape. Nevertheless, my family, knowing that I must have been in charge, went into the traditional nine days of mourning when they heard that we had all been killed.

All night we walked. When we got to Old Cape on Monday morning, Rufus was there. I had not seen him, but the boys delighted in scaring him by telling Rufus I was surely going to kill him. In truth, I would not have killed him, but I would have thrown him in jail. Rufus took off again.

We slept Monday night near Old Cape, then the next morning we walked the remaining three miles to our base at Twibila. The news of our victory and our trouble preceded us into Twibila, so when we walked into our base, there was a big celebration waiting for us. The children and the young boys all sang:

Man Wal Wamni
By Esteban (Chingo Lingo) Morze
Kaulkira, Honduras, 1983
(In Miskito)

Komandante Ráfaga man wal wamni
Man wal wamni
Wamni Bihmuna ra
Wam ni Sita-Awala ra
Wam ni Sandy Bay ra
Wam ni Yulo ra
Wam ni Ani Ani ra
Man wal wamni.

Mitham aihkikara
M16 kam aiwani sa *Rá–fa–ga*
Mitham smihkam ra
9-millimeter kam aiwani sa *Rá–fa–ga*

Karna sabibas, sabibas
Kan nahara kum tara kahwan na
Bukra sin wala tara kahwan ba
Kau uria kainam ra pat wala tara
Kum bata kram ba.

Mihtam wal sut wina
Lawana pain kira aiwani ba *Rá–fa–ga*
Kaisa sut aiwanaya Ráfaga
Man wal wamni.
Pura luwaya ba yawan dukiasa
¡Tawaswalpa pri apia kaka pruwaya!

We Will Go With You

Comandante Ráfaga we will go with you
We will go with you
We'll go to Bihmuna
We'll go to Sita-Awala
We'll go to Sandy Bay
We'll go to Yulo
We'll go everywhere with you.

In your right hand
Your M16 sings *Rá–fa–ga*
In your left hand
Your 9-millimeter sings *Rá–fa–ga*

Hit 'em hard!
One fell here
Another fell there
Beyond fell another
And all of them are falling.

From your hands
We hear the melody *Rá–fa–ga*
Let's all sing with you Ráfaga
Let's go! Victory is ours!
A free Atlantic Coast or death!

I was shot up and had a bad infection from the shoulder wound. My fever was high and my feet were hurting from ground itch. I could not even lift up my arms because I was so weak and hot with fever. That is how I was feeling when I went to Iralaya to meet with Fagoth, who was allied with the Honduran military and the remnants of the Somocista National Guard, to tell them about the details of our mission.

Well, Fagoth tried to flatter me, but I was in no mood for his foolishness and I was pretty mad at him too. Fagoth said to me, "Ráfaga, you are the right man. You are the brave man. You, Ráfaga, should be the big leader." I let him finish flattering me with those words, then I got mad and argued with him. I fought him with words: "The blood of my seven boys who lost their lives at Bihmuna is on your hands, Fagoth! The Sandinistas have good weapons, but the good weapons that we should have had you gave to the Honduran army!"

All the boys gathered around that place where I was fighting with Fagoth and they backed me up, every one of them. Fagoth told me he wanted to take me to a good doctor in Tegucigalpa, but I told him my boys were hurt and shot up just like me, and why should they be treated by less qualified physicians? I was hot mad! I said to Fagoth, "If you carry me to a good doctor in Tegucigalpa, then you must also carry every one of my boys who is shot to the same doctor! They deserve no less than me!" And so I compelled Fagoth to carry all of us to the hospital at Tegucigalpa where our injuries were treated and where I was hospitalized for one full month. After my release I went to a Honduran Miskito Indian village called Kaulkira, where I had to convalesce for four months. Some of my young boys rested with me.

I stayed in the house of the Reverend Moses Bendles. I want to speak about the Bendles family members because all of them helped me like a second family, and they deserve to be mentioned here and remembered always. Mr. and Mrs. Bendles had four daughters: the oldest was Ruth, next was Magda, then Norma, and the youngest was Myrna. All of the Bendles family treated me very nicely, especially Norma and Myrna. Also, Myrna's husband, Oliver Haylok, was always kind and helpful to me. When I remember these people, my heart is full of joy because they all loved me so much and supported me when I was in need of help.

The family gave me money and gave my boys money also. All that they did for me, they did for my boys. They gave us clothing, fed us, and took us to the doctor when we needed to see one.

All of the Bendles family members are Miskito Indian people. Moses Bendles is a Moravian minister in Kaulkira. Even though he is a Honduran Miskito and I am a Nicaraguan Miskito, we felt like we shared the same problems. I believe that was part of the reason why that family cared for me so well, as if they had been passing through big trouble like me. Or perhaps they believed that someday in the future a war would come to Honduras that would place them in the same kind of peril I was in then. It is my belief that sooner or later the Miskitos living in Honduras will have the same problem as we and will have to fight for their right to autonomy.

The reverend's daughter Magda worked in a health clinic, so she would bring medicine home to me and to my boys. I had malaria and chills in my bones. We caught the sickness in Twibila, I believe, because there are many mosquitoes and sand flies there, which bit us often and gave us a sickness like malaria.

I have not seen the Bendles family since that time, nor have I tried to write to them. Any communication from me could possibly bring suspicion on them from the Honduran government. I hope that someday the Bendles family will read this book and know that I feel so much love and respect for each one of them.

All of those people, the Bendleses and the Hayloks, could see the crookedness of Steadman Fagoth and how he was mistreating us guerrilleros. That is the reason why those two families arranged for me to become a naturalized Honduran. That task required much time and money in order to get the security clearance and good documents made for me.

Initially, I felt happy with this whole idea of staying in Honduras, but the boys were not content, and soon after they went back into the jungle at RusRus to train. I too was not content with the situation. All I could think of was my boys who were in the jungle; it did not seem right for me not to be with them.

Realizing that I could not abandon the boys, I went over to RusRus, which is ninety miles from Twibila and far into the mountainous interior of Honduras, where Fagoth had sent them to a training base. From RusRus I walked six miles to the base called Centro de Instrucción Militar (CIM).

When I arrived at CIM, I found my boys unhappy because Fagoth was forcing them to be trained by Somocista guardsmen—Somozan Spaniards who ran away to Honduras following the Triumph. Also, Fagoth was having plenty of big trouble with the Miskito guerrilla boys because they did not like living with and being trained by Spaniards.

Fagoth arranged for the guardsmen to kill many Miskito boys who made trouble. The boys made trouble only because we did not like Spaniards' being over us and we did not like Fagoth's being so closely connected to them. I will give you some examples of how Fagoth had some of the Miskito boys murdered by the Spaniards.

There were two Miskito brothers from Kum, on the Río Coco,

whose names were Asunción and Simon Waldan. Fagoth had those brothers killed because they asked for some of the food, clothing, and weapons that had been delivered by the CIA to Fagoth for the Miskito boys fighting the revolution. The Waldan brothers knew that $19 million had been allocated by the U.S. government and demanded that Fagoth deliver the supplies to the guerrillas. So Fagoth sent them out on a special mission and sent guardsmen out ahead with guns. Simon and Asunción were murdered in an ambush.

An example of the high level of discontent can be found in the struggle between two Miskito boys, Eduardo Kolman and his brother, and Fagoth. The Kolman brothers were always talking to the boys about their rights and showing how, despite all the money the United States was giving Fagoth, the boys had no supplies. The Kolman brothers asked Fagoth, "Where and for what is that money being spent? In Miami Beach for mansions and big cars for the Somocista big leaders?" Fagoth sent a group of guardsmen to arrest them, but they escaped. Afterward, the Kolman brothers found Fagoth and another MISURA big man called Wycliffe Diego eating and drinking at a sidewalk café called Las Perlas in Puerto Lempira. The brothers threw a grenade at Fagoth, but they were too far away; Fagoth was unhurt, and Diego's leg was injured a little. Fagoth sent the Honduran army after them. Fagoth was in business with the captain of the Honduran army, and because he had delivered so many arms and goods to them, he had a great deal of power. The Kolman brothers were captured and executed without trial.

That is the way it was done. There were plenty more Indian people who were murdered by Fagoth's orders—some Miskito, some Sumo. Many other bitter facts about Fagoth are important to this story, not because this book is about him, but because so much of what he did was the direct or indirect stimulus for the actions taken by me and the boys. Therefore, it is important that I make his actions known so our responses to his actions will be better understood.

After I had visited with my boys at CIM, I wanted to visit some Nicaraguan Miskito and Sumo people who were refugees in

Honduras. I had an interest to see how they were coming along. So I made a journey to many refugee camps. It bothered us that all those camps had Spanish names, like Puesto de Comando (Command Post).

After I had seen for myself what was happening to my Indian brothers and sisters living in those camps under Spanish authority, I went back to CIM to confront Fagoth. I took my Miskito boys out of that Spaniard base and we went into the mountains where we built our own guerrilla base in Honduras, which I named Miskut, in honor of the great Miskito *kasiki* who lived on the Atlantic Coast over four hundred years ago. We built another guerrilla base in Honduras, and I gave it the name Lakiatara, a Miskito word meaning " morning star." In Spanish they call it *lucero de la mañana*.

In July 1982 I came out from Miskut with about fifty Miskito boys. We went over into Nicaragua to Kum, where we fought the Sandinistas for about forty-five minutes. It was about nine o'clock in the morning when we finished the fight. Then we swam across the Río Coco back into Honduras and waited until night, when we swam across the river again into Nicaragua. Then we walked a road for two days, which brought us within ten miles of Bihmuna. There I heard that Comandante Blas, a Miskito Indian, had recently fought the Sandinistas in Bihmuna and burned two government trucks.

We caught up with Comandante Blas on August 10, 1982. He had with him twenty young Miskito boys. I gave Blas ten of my boys, which made his troops number thirty in all. I then had forty remaining with me.

Comandante Blas and I fought together against the Sandinistas on August 15, 1982, in Bilwaskarma, on the Río Coco. There we burned down one of the command posts, which was like a fort. Two of my boys were killed in that fight. Afterward, we all walked on toward Yulo.

While we were trying to get over to Yulo, we fought the Sandinistas in a place called Sannilaya. The date was August 21, 1982. In that fight, one Miskito boy was killed.

Next, I took my boys to the big mountain at Seven Benk, a Miskito village of only seven houses. On that mountain I put up a base of my own. The date was September 13, 1982. We stayed there for a little over two weeks, and from there we made one trip back to Kum for a fight.

No Indians were living in Kum. They had all been relocated. But there was livestock running wild all about the village because the inhabitants had been forced to leave the animals behind. Only pigs and Sandinistas were living there. Without notifying me, one of the boys shot a big pig, which was fine because it belonged to nobody. We tied its feet, then put it on a big stick to carry it back to camp with us. We were walking back along the rim of a hill when a group of Sandinistas from below spotted us. One of the boys was wearing a metal hat that looked like a fireman's hat, and when the Sandinistas began shooting at us, one of the bullets struck the hat and bored a hole right through it. Well, the boys were completely surprised by that attack. They let go of the pig, and the Miskito boy threw his metal hat onto the pig's head as they ran off into the bush to hide from the government soldiers.

Then the soldiers came up the hill to the spot where the boys had been, and all that was there was the pig on the stick wearing the metal hat with the bullet hole in it. The soldiers were frightened by what they saw. The boys watched and listened from the bush as the Sandinistas discussed what had happened: "Those guys are real witch men. This must be black magic. We shot an Indian and now he is a pig. We'd better get out of here! This place is cursed. Those black magic Indians will kill all of us." They didn't even take the pig as they ran off, so the boys retrieved it. We had a good meal and a good laugh.

There was a large patch of bush at Seven Benk, surrounded by flat, open grassland with a few pine trees here and there. We had church there: a pulpit where we could get up and pray. Along with us was a preacher from Krukira by the name of Tirelio Wilson.

On September 20, 1982, a Miskito boy I had to stand watch over the open country came to me around nine in the morning to report that some people were approaching us across the meadow. I went back to have a look and saw government soldiers coming on fast. They were already within half a mile. I quickly alerted the boys and we left the base to start fighting.

The Sandinistas had two women fighting along with them and a prisoner, a preacher, whom they later executed. After about four hours of fighting with our old and inadequate weapons, the two Sandinista women left their positions, ran over to us, and asked to join us. They turned their good weapons against the government soldiers and helped us to continue the fight. Reinforcements to the enemy had been arriving throughout the day, so we were in great danger.

When our Miskito preacher, Tirelio Wilson, saw what was happening, he got on his knees and started to pray. He told me later that while he was on his knees, God reminded him of "The 'Pistol' of the Apostle Paul." He immediately got up and started firing the little pistol he carried but had never used. He fought fiercely that day at Seven Benk. And later he said, "I had to do that to save my life!"

We fought that whole day, then when night came, we retreated and scattered ourselves about. For six days we were separated from each other. I tracked the movements of the government soldiers while my boys gradually found their way back to me. Another comandante called Tunki (Ignacio Salgado) was along with us as well. We fought a few small battles with the Sandinistas for three or four days as we chased them through the jungle.

After eight days had passed, we came across a farm where there were only Spanish Nicaraguans living and working. The man who was in charge of the farm told us, "You had better stay and rest yourselves here." We were all tired from chasing Sandinistas through the bush for so many days. None of us had eaten. My feet were sore with ringworm, too. So we took off our boots and put them up to dry while we all lay down in the yard by the house. I felt fairly confident that the Sandinistas we had been chasing would not turn back from their course. Our weapons were filthy, so while we were taking our rest, we broke our guns down and started cleaning them. I put a Miskito boy, who was barefoot and tired also, to stand guard. That boy fell asleep when he should have been watching for danger.

A neighbor turned out to be a Sandinista. He found the soldiers and reported on our position and our vulnerability. They turned back to attack us. They found the man on watch and slit his throat, then burst into the yard firing their weapons on us, barefooted and resting.

I counted thirty-four Sandinistas. We left four of them casualties. We had to leave behind the boy whose throat was cut— Timson Mateo, from my home town of Awastara. We did not have time to bury that Awastara boy, but just had to leave his body there for the jungle animals to pick his bones. All of us had to scatter quickly into the bush on our own. I was in the bush for fourteen days without eating anything except leaves and a few tree roots.

Some of the boys came out of the bush into Krukira while others came through Tuara. We finally joined together—sixteen boys with Comandante Tunki and twenty with me—at Pahara. There we counted our losses from the fight at the Spanish farm two weeks earlier—four dead, including Timson Mateo. One of the boys, William Preston, had been badly wounded in the hand and arm during that fight at the farm, and the wound had become seriously infected during the two weeks in the jungle. He had a high fever. I wanted to take him to Honduras to get medical treatment, but we barely had any ammunition left and needed to wait in Pahara for supplies. I had to make the decision to cut off William's arm. Yes, I gave that order to a man with us who knew a bit about medicine and cutting. He used a bayonet for the amputation. If we had not done it, William Preston would have died.

Before we had received more bullets from Honduras, a group of Sandinistas came to Pahara to attack us. I had to think deeply about how we could fight well with so few bullets. Pahara is an open place, so it is hard to defend. I decided that we should build a trench in the shape of a half-moon. I ordered Tunki and his gang into the trench and told them to hold fire until the Sandinistas got very close. Tunki and his sixteen boys waited, and as they opened fire, I took my twenty boys around the Sandinista line and divided them into four groups, which scattered out to attack. When we began shooting, the soldiers figured we were a big Contra reinforcement when in truth we were just four little groups of Miskito boys who had only a few bullets. But the soldiers believed as I had hoped and they began to run away.

We chased them to the edge of Awastara Lagoon, where many of them were hesitant to get into the water. We shot twenty-four Sandinistas there. Not one Miskito boy was killed, and I feel proud and grateful for that.

You see, when we have a straight line of soldiers coming into us like that, we force them with our half-moon–shaped trench into a curved line. This places them in a position that makes it possible to threaten them from the front and from behind. I learned that strategy fighting in the bush. There is much to be learned from the animal and bird voices, from the trees and the singing of the wind. That is how I was taught these ways. It is true.

We were in Pahara ten days waiting for our supplies to arrive from Honduras. All of the boys were running out of shoes and clothes. Many were almost naked. So the people of Pahara organized a collection of things the boys needed and gave them enough that when they had cleaned themselves up, they looked pretty nice. That made them start to look around in Pahara for girlfriends.

I set up a base six miles north of Sandy Bay, where Comandante Sutum was already camped. He and I traveled around to recruit Miskito boys to fight with us, and then we spent November and December 1982 training them how to fight. I made a trip in early December to Awastara to visit my mother, whom I had not seen for two years. While in Honduras or fighting in the bush, I had sent messages to her by way of Miskitos traveling in that direction to let her know where I was and that I was all right. During that visit to my home village, I was treated very well. They gave me new shoes and clothes. All this encouraged me in the work I was doing.

After we got back to our base at Sandy Bay, I traveled north to talk to some of the Miskito boys who had been watching the movements of the Sandinistas in the area. They told me that the government was preparing to bring soldiers into the Sandy Bay area by helicopter. I went back to the base to get the boys ready to fight. Our supplies had finally arrived, and for the first time we had good arms and enough bullets. The boys were healthy, too, because the Sandy Bay people had been feeding them good fish from the lagoon. I believed that they were ready to fight.

We dug a trench and burned out all the tall grass so we could see when the soldiers were coming to attack us.

The boys were right about the impending attack. On December 18, 1982, two helicopters flew in and put forty soldiers down on the ground to attack us. Our Miskito boys numbered forty-seven. I took charge of twenty-seven of them and Comandante Sutum took the rest. We used the same half-moon trench strategy that we had used at Pahara.

I put some of the boys in the trench while the others hid on a big pine ridge before the helicopters arrived. I had told them, "We never had good arms or so many bullets before, and we had to run around to escape the Sandinistas. Now you can get your revenge. Anyone that tries to leave or run away, I will shoot! Be brave men now!" I also instructed them to shoot first at the radio operators and the officers.

The boys followed my orders exactly. They got the radio operator and the officers early on in the fight. There was no way for the soldiers to contact their base or get reinforcements from Puerto Cabezas.

We started fighting at one in the afternoon. By three, numerous Sandinistas were dead. We kept on fighting. One of my officers, Munos Wilfred, got killed in that fight, and another, whom we called Tapite, was wounded in the back. When night came down on us, we stopped fighting and swam across the river, then walked toward the seashore. We walked along the beach all the way back to Honduras.

As we passed by Bihmuna on my personal road by the sea, the one I always used, I remembered the boys I had buried at the seashore nine months earlier. I was curious to see whether the Sandinistas had dug them up and thrown them away, because they liked to do things like that to the Indians. So when we arrived at that special place on the beach, I took those three boys out of their graves just to make sure their resting places had not been disturbed. I found Jaime, Barquero, and Flat Nose exactly as I had placed them. They looked no different, only dried up. The following day we continued along the shore to Honduras.

For a few months I stayed in Iralaya, Honduras, where I trained some Miskito boys who had come from Sandy Bay. In March 1983 Comandante Sutum came to take over the training while I went to Tegucigalpa. I stayed there for a couple of months until the intelligence division of MISURA brought the news that the Sandinistas were back in Old Cape. I decided to go back to Iralaya to prepare the boys for battle again. We began fighting at Old Cape on September 20, 1983.

We followed the Sandinistas to a house where many government soldiers were hiding. We killed and wounded many. I was shot seriously in the left leg. I could not walk, so my boys carried me on their backs to Honduras, and then MISURA sent me to Hospital Escuela in Tegucigalpa.

I stayed three days in the hospital. The doctors all told me my leg could not be saved. They told me I would die if it were not amputated. The director of the hospital came to visit me one day, and I told her not to let them cut off my leg. And they never did cut it off. Because I protested, I am now walking on two legs.

I believe many of those doctors had not studied well. Many of our boys lost their legs to Honduran doctors.

While I was in Hospital Escuela, plenty of the nurses started to fall in love with me. I was told that they cried when I left at five o'clock one morning against medical advice on the day they had scheduled my surgery. When I left, I was wearing my hospital gown and my military boots.

One young doctor there whom I liked very much was Mercedes Vanegas. She saw me not just as a patient but as a young man who could be loved. We both felt strong love for each other, and after I left the hospital we continued to be in love.

I stayed at the Hotel Lempira for a week and then at the Hotel Imperial. I was invited often to Mercedes Vanegas's house, and we enjoyed each other's company about the city while our friendship grew for many months.

It became necessary for me to spend time away from Tegucigalpa because I had to travel to many secret Contra bases. But after each trip I would return to the capitol to see Mercedes. I was deeply in love with that doctor—she was twenty-seven— and she loved me also. She was very good to me, friendly and gentle in her ways. I believe she would have been a good wife and mother also. But the circumstances of my life in the war caused us to be separated when it was time for me to go back to fight against the Sandinistas. That parting was a sad one.

THE COOLING ON MUKU

The doctors at the hospital had told me that I could not keep fighting because my leg bone was mashed up badly and would no longer support my weight and the heavy weapons I had to carry into battle. Many others tried to convince me not to go back to fighting for the revolution. I began to think deeply about my future and my past, which had been filled with too many accidents and dangers.

I felt like I needed some time to reflect on my circumstances so I could make a decision about my future. I went to Puerto Cortés, Honduras, where a cousin, Alan Hammer, was a manager in a factory called Zona Libre. There I began writing down all of the experiences of my life. I believed I should try to quit the war and that by writing my history on paper I would be able to judge the meaning of my past activities and make a correct decision.

So in November of 1983 I was in Puerto Cortés writing my history and trying not to think too much about what my Miskito boys were doing. But they always came back into my thoughts. I always remembered their courage as they were fighting for their freedom, for their rights, and for the liberty of the Miskito people. Even as I sat there safely in Puerto Cortés, I knew that my boys were somewhere fighting hard, and that made me feel guilty.

Tirelio Wilson and other leaders of MISURA came to Puerto Cortés on December 6, 1983, and found me at my cousin's house. They told me that my boys needed me and that the MISURA leaders wanted me to come back to work. I went to Tegucigalpa to meet with Steadman Fagoth. He asked me to lead a mission called Alpha Uno. Feeling compelled to oblige his request, I left immediately for La Ceiba, then two days later took a plane to Puerto Lempira, Honduras. I arrived at RusRus, where many of my boys were waiting for me. Several comandantes as well were there to welcome me back.

The following day we talked about the Alpha Uno mission, which I was to make into Nicaragua. I was to take 160 boys and men on a very important political mission. Although many of the men were older than I, I was to be in charge.

When I came out of CIM on December 7, 1983, I was not feeling very confident about my leg. It still hurt from time to time. Without the extra weight of weapons and ammunition, I felt pretty good, but when I put on all my gear I realized it would be much more difficult than ever before. Around my waist I had two hundred bullets in my belt and more in my *muchila* (backpack). I also carried a canteen, some food, a hammock, and a poncho—about fifty pounds in all.

The first day walking, this extra fifty pounds did not bother me too much. But after five days walking, it all got very heavy. Many times I wished I could just take off everything. Not even one small bullet did I want to carry. You have to have balls to carry all that gear through the jungle for ten or twelve days!

Even our boots and clothes get heavy because they are nearly always wet. We were always passing through swamps and rivers. The Atlantic Coast is not a pleasant place to be a guerrilla. Because of the wetness, many guerrilla boys do not like to wear underwear. Wet drawers bruise your crotch and can give you ringworm and groin itch. I use only women's underwear of the thin black nylon sort. They have thin seams around the legs so they do not bother the legs and crotch too much. Because they are black they hide the dirt. That is important because sometimes we guerrillas cannot take a shower or wash our clothes for several weeks. Because they are nylon they are quick to dry. Someday if someone sees me wearing women's underwear, they must not be frightened or see me as peculiar.

So, as we walked out of CIM on December 7, we had only our mission in mind, but much more than Alpha Uno lay ahead. From RusRus, we walked to a place by the name of Fransa, an Indian village at the edge of the Río Coco on the Honduran side. We gave some food to the Honduran soldiers there because they only had oranges to eat. I sent some of my boys to kill game and they brought back deer and peacock. The next day Fagoth brought food, bullets, and a cow.

In Fransa we got little canoes that carried us to a village called San Alberto, where it is pure big bush. Our mission was to go to Francia Sirpe, Nicaragua, which is a three-day walk from San Alberto; however, I had a premonition that the road there had been mined by the Sandinistas, so we took a course northeast forty-five degrees. This meant three extra days of walking. But what should have been a six-day trek turned out to be a nine-day journey because while we were on that route, we came very close to a sacred hill that the old Miskitos call Muku Hill. I wanted to go and have a look at the mysterious mountain. On December 13 we left the trail to climb Muku Hill.

Nobody I know has ever gone into Muku Hill. I had only been told about the sacred place by old Indians who had heard about it from someone before. A few people know about Muku, but they do not go there because they are afraid. I believe God sent me to Muku to prepare my soul for Alpha Uno, the mission that was to be the most difficult of my lifetime. For that mission to be successful, I had to be completely annealed. Up until that time on the road to Francia Sirpe when I first saw Muku from afar, my soul had only been heated by the many battles I had seen and had been made brittle by all the death and destruction I had witnessed. I believed God knew what lay ahead in my journey and that He also knew that I, like a brittle piece of iron that had only been hammered and heated, now needed to be tempered by His cooling spirit inside Muku Hill. This would make the leader in me more malleable and the soul inside of me more sensitive to great demands and capable of extension.

By that process of annealing, I became the comandante who was equal to the task required by Alpha Uno.

The experience I had on Muku Hill was something deep. I want to bring it out of my memory so I can impart to you the richness and meaningfulness of it. It is difficult for me to do this, however, because many of the feelings and thoughts that were born in me by that experience were strange and unfamiliar. It is hard to find words to describe them all. Basically, I can say that I was saturated with God's presence and with the presence of many ancient Indian spirits in Muku Hill. I think, maybe, that I was made strong in my spirit by the presence of God on Muku, like Moses in the presence of the burning bush on Mount Sinai.

We had been several days without food as we walked along that trail to Francia Sirpe. When I saw that big mountain far off in the distance, I felt compelled to go to it. So I gave orders to my 160 boys to leave the trail and start walking toward Muku. That was on December 13.

It was not an easy climb, and many of the boys could not understand my motive for wanting to go to the mountain when we were already behind schedule. I only knew that something strange was compelling me to go there.

The higher we climbed up Muku's steep slopes, the cooler the climate became. There was bountiful food, and the boys filled their empty bellies with sweet bananas, plantain, and cocoa. They also killed some peacock and deer, which we cooked and ate with much pleasure. After great patience and sweet struggle, we arrived at the top of Muku. From there we could see all of the nice view afar. We bathed in a stream of cool, clear water. It seemed to us, from the big boulders we found strewn all around the top, that Muku must have been a volcano. Some of the boulders looked to weigh fifty tons or more. But the rocks were stacked and divided too neatly. I told my boys that was some kind of work of God. He fixed it like this. That was the idea in my mind, but it was not my idea. It seemed to me to be God's idea.

I had a peculiar feeling that I did not want to come down from that place, but I knew that I must, so we began climbing down. Night caught us halfway down the slope and there we slept. I wanted to start down again early, around five, but not until eight could we see daylight through that heavy bush. When we finally got to the base of the great mountain, the boys were very tired and it was hot. They were frightened by the mountain and wanted to leave. Just then I remembered that one of the old heads had told me a legend about a tunnel into Muku Hill. I had not remembered that before, so I told the boys that something supernatural was putting that memory into my head just at that moment and that we should look for the tunnel. The boys were even more frightened by this and protested. But I was comandante, so I ordered twelve of the boys to come with me and the rest to wait for our return.

We had been walking around the base of Muku for two miles, and as we walked we saw many little holes in the side of the mountain, but they did not seem to have any particular significance to me. Then suddenly by body felt totally different. I felt cold and shivered, but the air was warm all around me. I stopped walking and just stood quietly for a few minutes. Then a sweet smell, like perfume, surrounded us. The twelve boys smelled it, too, and were scared. I started walking in the direction where the sweet smell seemed to be strongest. The boys would not follow.

Then my feet stopped walking. I sensed a powerful presence, like someone was near my side, but I saw nothing. Next, as I stood motionless, I sensed many, many Indian spirits all around me, but in combination their energy was less than the One that was at my side. I felt uncomfortable and a little afraid because it was a very unfamiliar situation. Then, for an instant that seemed to be outside time, I felt completely separated from all of my earthly sensations, like I was suspended in nothingness. Next, I began to feel once again connected to my senses. I remember looking about and smelling the air around me. At the same time, I became aware that I was no longer uncomfortable or afraid. Instead I felt greatly protected and calm, moving forward in an attitude of purpose and expectation. I had only taken a few steps when there was indeed before my eyes a hole in the side of the mountain, which I knew was the tunnel the old heads had mentioned. I called out to the boys, "I have found it! Come! Let's go see for ourselves this legend." But the boys did not come.

I entered the hole with my flashlight, willing to go in alone. After I had taken a few steps inside, I could hear the boys moving about the entrance, so I returned to them and said, "In the ancient days, the Indians lived here. You must not be afraid. I have heard about this tunnel from the old heads, and we are fortunate to be here to see it for ourselves. This is an important mission we have here, so even if you are frightened, you must come with me to witness this place. Even if we all die, we will die as brave guerrilla warriors. We are revolutionaries, and because we are, we do not mind if we die on a mission. Let's go on in!"

My boys came in behind me after I explained the importance of this mission. We had walked about three hundred yards, looking around with our flashlights, when we came to a big room that contained twelve chairs carved into the rock and a stone pulpit like an altar. The rock was the color of chocolate and it was very clean and shiny. Some of the rock looked and felt slick.

On the walls of the big room I saw, with my own eyes, markings carved into the rock. Some of the markings looked like letters, but if it was a language, I could not understand its meaning. Also carved into the rock were pictures of big mountain cows, snakes, deer, and eagles. There were also prints in human form, carved stone figures that looked like idols, and pots of various sizes, some with pictures on them, which they must have used for cooking and storing food.

I could not recognize some of the animals represented by the markings and carvings, so I believe they do not exist now. I knew that what I was seeing must have been made many thousands of years ago, perhaps five or six thousand years ago.

As I stood in the big room where the chairs and altar were, I began to see in my mind's eye and to feel in my spirit that the ancient Indians had used the place for ritual worship. I noticed that the chairs were very small. I tried to sit in one of them but could not fit into it. I looked closely at the markings on the walls and noticed that some of them were very narrow and that they would gradually become wider as they went along.

I am not a scientist, but I began to understand that big Indian leaders—*kasikis*—had sat in those chairs, done rituals, and worshiped. I saw it happening in my mind as though I were living back then, many thousands of years ago. It was beautiful! My soul was filled with exquisite joy as those visions passed before my eyes. It was a different group of Indians that I saw— not Miskito—and they had great power. They were big like me, so I wondered how they had fit into those small chairs.

Then I began to feel life in the room. Not the life of man but the life of Muku. Yes, I felt the life in the mountain all around me. The walls, the chairs, and the ceiling all seemed to breathe like a living thing. I felt that Muku was trying to explain its secrets to me, trying to answer my questions about the smallness of the chairs, the largeness of the room, and the discrepancies in the size of the mysterious markings. I believe that this life I felt was causing the chairs to shrink and the room to grow larger. I am filled with awe as I imagine how this could be so, and I cannot explain it further. It is too big for a human mind to consider.

Every place inside of that big room was very clean, whereas the tunnel leading to the big room was dirty in places and scattered with broken pots all about. But in that great room it was clean and tidy. Also, the pots sitting about in the big room were whole, not in pieces like the ones in the passageway. It is my thinking that those ancient Indian spirits that I felt around me secretly keep the big room clean and neat. Yes, and I believe that those ancient *kasikis* did fit into those chairs in the ancient days, but since then the chairs have shrunk, so it was not possible for me to sit in them. Yes, the space filling the room had expanded, causing the chairs and the altar to shrink into a smaller form. That process had occurred because Muku is alive, breathing with life. I do not know the origin of that life, but it is life in the largest meaning of the word.

I have also had the thought that those ancient men buried great treasures in Muku and protect them there to this day.

We remained inside the mountain for about eight hours or so. I looked at everything in the big room very carefully and concentrated deeply because I knew that I was seeing things no living man had seen, and I realized the great importance of that experience.

That night of December 14, 1983, we slept at the foot of Muku, where the boys awaiting our return had made a camp.

As I prepared myself for sleep, many thoughts about the history of my people filled my head. I recalled what the old heads had told me about our ancestors—that they believed in many, many gods, such as the sun, the moon, and the morning star. They never knew about God like I had been taught. They called the god of the morning star Lakiatara. They liked to live alongside rivers and lakes so they could see the moon and stars in the water and feel that the gods lived there beside them and helped their crops grow.

It must have been another kind of Indian that worshiped in Muku. I wondered as I lay there next to the mountain under the stars that night if that other kind of Indian believed—as do the old Rama, Sumo, and Miskito people who go to live by a creek or river—that the closeness of the stars was making their crops grow well and not realize that it was the richness of the soil at the banks that accounted for their bountiful food. They must have thought that a god was living in those rivers and bringing them good crops because they could see the reflection shining up from the water.

When our ancestors found fire, they thought they had invented another god and worshiped fire. They did that for thousands and thousands of years. With the fires they made by striking rocks against each other, they were able to boil fish and roast meat. It was not easy to make a fire by striking rocks against each other, so they would protect the blaze so it could be used again and again. Some old people have told me that someone among the living Miskitos still protects that original flame, which has been burning since the ancient days. And many of us still live much like those people, carrying our things in little boats on the rivers, settling briefly on the banks of rivers, farming and fishing, and raising our children in those old ways.

I also thought about the stone idols I saw inside Muku. That made me wonder about the religion of the ancient people compared to my own religious beliefs and the beliefs of other present-day Indians. Many Indians still worship false idols, practice witchcraft, and go to the *brujo* (witch doctor) for assistance with problems. In the old days, the *curanderos* (healers) and *brujos* cured with medicines from the bush. And many still believe they can cure you and harm you. Some of the *brujos* are prophets. They know when hurricanes are coming and where gold and oil can be found. They know what will become of you in the future and if your wife is being faithful to you. And if you are sick, they can take out the sickness and give you a protection for your health.

But many of us are Christians now, so some of our old thinking has changed to this new way of believing in only one true God. When the Christian religion came to the coast more than 150 years ago, the Miskito, Sumo, and Rama Indians still believed in stone gods and in Lakiatara.

The Moravian missionaries from Germany, North America, and Jamaica came and taught us about Jesus and the Bible and other documents, which proved to us that there is only one true God. Never before had we seen evidence for God like this. The Moravians also treated us well and gave us medicine. This convinced many of us that their ways and beliefs were superior to our old ways. This is why many left their old ways of thinking and believed what the Moravians taught us with their books and documents.

It seemed to me that those Indians who worshiped in Muku thousands of years ago may have written about their gods, too, but I cannot be sure because I could not understand the meaning of the markings I had seen on the walls and the pots inside Muku.

As I kept pondering these things, I realized that a great amount of time and history had occurred before the Miskito kingdom. I began to piece together what I had been taught in my life with what I had seen inside Muku.

The Bible says that from the time of Adam and Eve to the time of Noah two thousand years passed. Then, from the time of Noah to Sodom and Gomorrah two thousand years more passed. From Sodom until the crucifixion of Christ, another two thousand years. And from then until now, it has been two thousand more. I calculated that it had been eight thousand years since the time God made man. I know that in reality time is incalculable. It is possible that millions of years could have passed actually, because the Bible says there can be a thousand years in a day. My spirit was quickened with an appreciation for all of life, for all of history, and for man's yearning for life through the centuries. Suddenly I felt very small compared to all that had preceded my existence, and yet I felt myself to be an extension of all that history. This humbled me as never before.

I wondered if other great sacred mountains of which the old heads had spoken held secrets inside them like this great Muku, high above the falls of the Río Coco. There is a giant hill called Sani Hill (Fiber Hill) about two thousand feet high near Siuna, another called Cola Blanca (White Tail) near the town of Bonanza, and near Yulo, there are two more, Tilba Hill (Cow Mountain) and Prata Hill (Old Mountain). Similar legends of treasure and ancient ritual are told about all these mountains.

There are also stories of great battles that were fought by the old race to protect those mountains and the treasures inside. Those were not Miskitos, but were perhaps the same ancient tribe that made the chairs and place of worship in Muku. I believe that our Miskito Indians came to the Atlantic Coast of Central America much later from the south. I think we originated in what is now Colombia. I have heard that a number of Miskito words are also place names in Colombia. There are villages in Colombia, whose names have meanings in the Miskito language, for example, Cucuta ("top of the coconut") and Bukuramango ("mango fruit there").

I considered all these things that night and many other questions, such as: How did the humans who were made by God in Eden, which was in Africa, eventually get to Central and South America? How did man, who was black, eventually come to be white and yellow and brown? Why are some people in the world strong and others weak?

The Bible had taught me that after Adam and Eve were created they fell from grace, then started to multiply and scattered out after making the Tower of Babel. But how did these people get to where I live, and why is my color different?

I have an idea that those people were created in Africa and then they spread out. Some went to Asia and others went to different places throughout the world. Those who stayed in Africa remained black because of the hot climate. In Asia, because of the cold climate, they got whiter. And the Indians around here have become brown like me because of the climate and the food we eat. It is my idea that whoever stays in the house, for reason of climate or occupation, gets lighter skinned. There are differences in color among my own people—between fishermen and farmers. Those who fish get black and burned with salt water. They shrivel up, their eyes get weak and they get old quick. But those who stay in the house do not get black. In Awastara we do not get very black or get old too fast. But those who have made a trip on the high seas have turned black already by the time they come back. Also, when a man comes back from the high seas and makes a baby, that baby turns out a little darker than the father.

After seeing all that evidence of ancient people in Muku, I thought about the progression of all those generations that have come down, down, down through the ages, and I believe that our color has been changed by degrees for the reasons I have given. That is why, many years ago, African people got to be black and people of other nations got to be white.

I also thought about why some people in different parts of the world are strong and others are weak. Here on the Atlantic Coast of Nicaragua, we Indians eat plenty of fish, seafood, and turtle, so we are stronger and healthier than those on the Pacific Coast, who do not eat these foods. Those Pacific Coast people drink a liquor made from grain corn called *pinolio*, which we do not drink. So I think that food may have an influence on our general health. We here on the Atlantic Coast look young longer and, in truth, live longer lives than those people on the

Pacific Coast. There are many people I know on the Atlantic Coast—both men and women—who are more than a hundred years old.

These are some of the many things I speculated about that night. I believe that all this thinking affected my soul in such a way that I discovered a new attitude in myself, a thoughtfulness regarding my life, the reason for my existence, the purpose of my future, and a new desire to survive—not just my own survival, but the survival of every human being. I awakened with that attitude on December 15, 1983, and it was with enhanced sensitivity in my soul, an acute mind, and a deep respect for all human life, past and present, that I left Muku Mountain and led my boys into Francia Sirpe, where Mission Alpha Uno began. Had I not had that experience in Muku, I doubt that I would have managed the mission as I did. I was a different man, a leader whose soul and mind functioned in perfect harmony to make the unerring decisions that brought me, my boys, three thousand Indians, two deacons, a priest, and a Catholic bishop safely through the most critical trial of my life: Mission Alpha Uno.

Eight / Matlalkahbipurawal

Alpha Uno: The Bishop, Moses, and Me

Alpha Uno was a political mission designed by the CIA and Steadman Fagoth. A Cuban-American working for the CIA helped plan the mission, which I was to lead. That CIA man was called Alex—I do not know if that was his legal name. I now know that he was CIA because I have read this information in *Libro Unico* (see chapter nine). He had come to CIM to make the plan for Alpha Uno. In a meeting at Fagoth's house Eduardo Pantin, Fagoth, Alex, and others designated Francia Sirpe as the place where the mission would originate. After that meeting Alex explained to me how the mission was to be carried out and what goals were to be achieved.

Alpha Uno was not designed to be a military mission. It was designed to be what we call "political work"; in truth, however, it turned out to be as great a military mission as it was political. The original plan called for me to take 160 Miskito warriors to Francia Sirpe. Once there, we were to convince all the village people to walk to Honduras as a sign of protest against the Sandinista government. It was our hope, and the hope of the CIA, that a protest demonstration the size and magnitude of Alpha Uno would alert the world to what was happening in Nicaragua to the Miskito, Rama, and Sumo nations, and would result in additional material and lethal aid for the revolutionaries who were fighting to regain the rights of the Indian people.

It was three o'clock on the afternoon of December 18, 1983, when we stopped about half a mile from Francia Sirpe. I sent five MISURA scouts led by an Indian fellow called Walker into

118

the village to find out whether any Sandinista troops were present. Later Walker and his boys returned and reported no Sandinista guards or military.

I moved my troops into the village that night, arriving at about eight o'clock. After we had gotten well inside the village, an uneasy feeling came over me, which caused me to question the correctness of the intelligence report. There was an unexplained tension among the people. Their expressions were fearful and guarded. I felt that we needed more information, so we captured a boy who was about fifteen, and that boy showed me three houses in the village where Sandinista men were hiding. The boy told me that in addition to the Spanish Sandinistas there were two Miskito Indians who were sympathetic to the Sandinista government. Their names were Richard and Slipers. The boy also reported that the government teachers in the village, together with the Sandinistas, numbered twenty-eight and that all were well armed.

My boys were angered that those two Miskitos, Richard and Slipers, had joined the Sandinistas. As we walked cautiously into the village with our weapons ready, the Miskito, Richard, started shooting at us from his house. The boys quickly retaliated with a volley of automatic fire. That fight had started without my order. By the time I arrived at Richard's house and realized what had happened, I quickly gave the boys orders not to shoot anymore at anyone. I told them that Richard was Miskito like us and that we should not take the life of a brother no matter what his politics might be.

The moon was full and shining happily. It was so bright that night that I could see all parts of the village. After those initial shots were fired into Richard's house, the village people began running out of their houses to see what was happening. Many were creeping low on the ground because they were so frightened.

The boys surrounded Richard's house. It was a high house atop stilts, so some of the boys went under the floor. It was then that the wife shouted to us that Richard had been shot bad, so the boys forced their way into the house, took hold of the wounded Richard, dragged him out of the house, and began kicking him. When I saw the boys start to kick Richard, I was close by, so I gave orders for them to stop. I walked over to look on my wounded brother and saw that he was shot badly.

The people of the village came to tell me what a bad man Richard was. All those people wanted me to kill him. Also, the wife of that bad fellow came to me saying she had always advised him not to be involved in political business with the Sandinista but that he had told her he intended to die working with the government.

I gave Richard some antibiotics and some medicine to diminish the pain, then I told his wife that it seemed Richard would die unless she could get him to the hospital in Puerto Cabezas. It was my intention to take everyone out of Francia Sirpe—not to leave one person there. But I did tell the wife of Richard that she would be allowed to stay behind to mind him and to try to take him to the hospital in Port. But she did not want to do that. She wanted to go with the others to Honduras.

Richard's mother came to me asking if she could remain behind to care for him. I gave her some medicine and explained how she might carry him to Port for treatment.

We do not seek to kill any of our Miskito people. Not one Indian from the coast has ever perished by my hand or by my order.

The Indian called Slipers, who was also working for the Sandinistas, came to me to turn himself in and to give up his pistol. Then all the government teachers and the Sandinista men, who were elderly but well armed, came like Slipers and turned in their weapons.

I did not want any more shedding of blood in that little place.

The total population of the community was about three thousand. At ten o'clock that night the boys and I began organizing the people for the long walk to Honduras. All were willing and ready to leave.

The boys gathered provisions from the government food storage houses and gave each family a ration to carry. We took milk, flour, rum, and medicine for the journey. We also took six cows from the village. Many of the three thousand Indians took with them individual rations and food for their children.

A few minutes after ten o'clock on the night of December 18, 1983, we and the three thousand started to move out of Francia Sirpe and onto the road to Honduras.

I had a group of thirty men with me. We went ahead of the three thousand to a little town called Tronquera. Our mission there was to bomb a bridge so the Sandinistas would not be able to follow us. I was worried about the many civilians I was leading to Honduras, and I was thinking deeply about their safety and their lives. That is why we bombed the Tronquera bridge. The idea, to blow up the bridge, came from Comandante Papaya (Ismael Ramos).

Soon after we had finished with that bridge at Tronquera, four men wearing religious clothes and tennis shoes came to the place where I was on the road. The four looked like Catholic religious people. Two were white men whom I did not recognize, but the two Miskito Indians I recognized as Deacon Francisco Baker and Deacon Isidoro Mercado, Catholic missionaries from the Atlantic Coast. One of the white men was big and fat and tall. He must have weighed over 250 pounds. He told me that his name was Salvador Schlaefer and that he was the Catholic bishop of Zelaya. The other white man was a Catholic priest by the name of Wendelin Shafer. Those two told me that they and the two Miskito missionaries wanted to go along with me and the three thousand to Honduras as a sign of the church's agreement with this political mission.

I told the bishop, "With those light tennis shoes, you cannot walk to Honduras. The journey is long and there is plenty of mud and rock to pass through." The bishop protested, believing that he was capable of making the journey. Over and over again, he begged to go with me and the others to Honduras.

The bishop told me about a problem he and the people of Santa Clara had with the Sandinista government. Juan Solorzano ("Laihn Pihni," White Lion), who was comandante with me on Mission Alpha Uno, had made a similar mission with the Santa Clara people. On that mission, the religious people had chosen not to go to Honduras and had stayed behind. After the Indians of Santa Clara had gone with Solorzano to Honduras, the Sandinistas had come to Santa Clara and had persecuted and jailed many of the Catholic religious people in that community, believing they had caused the Indians to leave. Now, in Francia Sirpe, the bishop anticipated a similar situation, so he did not want to remain behind as he had done in Santa Clara earlier that year. From the time of that problem, they had decided to have no confidence in the government, nor to look forward to any improvement in their condition. He told me that since having had that problem in Santa Clara, the Sandinistas started to believe that not all of them were engaged in missionary or preaching work, but that the bishop and the priests were conspiring with the guerrillas to organize the people against the government. Also, that bishop enticed me to his way of thinking by telling me that our mission would have more weight and more coverage in the world press were he and the other three to go along with us, proclaiming their agreement with our political ideas.

Well, after all that discussion and debate, I decided to try to find some military boots for those four men. The bishop had big feet and we could not find any boots to fit him, but for the others we found some military boots. Those religious people had a Toyota four-wheel-drive vehicle, which we used to carry our provisions on ahead of the multitude, and for that contribution to our mission we were very thankful.

It was an incredibly great sight to see those three thousand Indians—men young and old, women and young girls, little children of all sizes, and babies in their mothers' arms—walking together with dignity and honor, proclaiming to all the world that we Miskito Indians did not want any more punishment from the Sandinista government, that we wanted our rights to be given back to us. And the religious men comforted the people as they walked along the road. The bishop always prayed for our safety and for the success of the mission. Soon it became apparent to me that those religious people, along with the comandantes, were the glue that held it all together.

But even they in their divine wisdom and we in our jungle savvy could not have made that journey a success without the direct intervention and protection of our God. It was a perilous journey that became more and more dangerous with each passing hour, but it was a great journey and a powerful political statement to the world that will be remembered in the history books. Future generations will know and understand the trouble we Miskitos were passing through during that time of December in the year 1983.

All night we walked. When daylight shone down on our faces we had arrived at a place called Wisconsin, an abandoned Miskito village inside the Nicaraguan border. That was the morning of December 19. I stayed close to the religious people because I felt responsible for their safety and well-being. Some of our boys had told the bishop, "Comandante Ráfaga and Comandante Laihn Pihni will be responsible for you. Our two head leaders will carry out this mission and bring us all to safety."

After we had passed through Wisconsin at five o'clock in the morning, Comandante Laihn Pihni, with eighty men, chose a road he believed to be abandoned. I, also with eighty men, followed far behind. I ordered twenty of my men to guard and protect the bishop and other religious people as they walked the road. We walked in that formation until two o'clock in the afternoon, when we came to the foot of a hill in the road we were traveling. There we rested for the first time since leaving Francia Sirpe. It began to rain heavily, and the multitude was tired and wet. We killed three of the six cows, and roasted and divided the meat among the people. Each person got one small piece of meat. There we passed the night about one kilometer behind the rest, to guard them from behind.

The following day, December 20, at about five o'clock in the morning, the boys started to get up, move around, and prepare some food for the religious people. I was so tired that I continued to lie in my hammock with my boots off. Immediately I put on my boots and told the boys that they must try to get ready because the enemy was near us.

The jungle was especially dense in that area. It was so thick that I could not see the sunrise, nor the sky, nor any light at all. I sent some of the boys to bring water from a place a few hundred feet away and told them, "You must watch out for yourselves because our enemy is near." But the boys did not believe me. One said, "There is no problem nor any enemy camp around us now."

When those boys got down to where the water was, the enemy was waiting there and began to fire at them. The boys dove into the water and swam safely to the other side. When I heard the gunfire, I took some of the other boys there, and we fought the Sandinistas for about fifteen minutes. None of us got hurt and none of the Sandinistas were hurt that I know about.

Then we advanced to where Laihn Pihni and the three thousand had camped, but when we got there, we found that they had left already. So I took the boys back to where the water was to look for the enemy. We could find no Sandinistas there. At about seven-thirty that morning one of my officers came to me saying, "Let's leave this place and catch up to Laihn Pihni and the others so we can continue with our journey." That officer's name was Cara Piedra (Rock Face). Comandante Papaya, who was with our group, also wanted to move out to join the others. But I told them, "A man that can be thinking ahead for the future is better than he who can think only for the present. That man who can think in the future is very important. So you must respect my thinking and my decision to stay here until we have found our enemy."

At exactly five minutes before eight o'clock, I lay down alone beneath the arching roots of a big *ceiba* (kapok) tree, where I spoke to its soul for assistance. That kind of tree is sacred to guerrillas because it gives us secret knowledge when we are in need.

In the bush we learn many mysterious things. Sometimes we become scientists through our secret Indian practices. With the jungle all around me, I can hear a different language. It is mysterious. With the many pretty birds that sing, I can listen to the meaning of their songs and more or less judge something to be important or not. Some of the bird songs tell me, "That is dangerous what you are about to do," and some say to me, "You must not go on that road because it is dangerous." Other bird songs tell me, "You must not sleep here," or they may say, "Get up and move off because your enemy is coming." A man with a good and true purpose, trying to live with a good conscience through his Indian courage, can learn many secrets from the jungle. If we respect nature, she will help us. We have great confidence in nature. That is how I believe, and that is the way it was.

That is why on the morning of December 20, 1983, at five minutes before eight o'clock, I went under the big ceiba tree and put my head between its massive roots, which were partly above the ground. In that way I concentrated to hear the strange thoughts that great tree put into my mind. I heard something from the tree that seemed like a group of people walking far ahead and another group of people coming toward me. The tree filled my mind with many ideas. As I sought its help, knowledge came to me right away.

I interpreted the beautiful language of the tree and immediately told my guerrilla boys that the enemy was very close. I described exactly where we would find them. I told the boys to prepare themselves to fight. They did not believe that I had received this knowledge from a tree, but they followed my orders to make themselves ready for battle. Fifteen minutes later, we found our enemy exactly where the tree had told me they were, and we received them in a very fine military way.

Those Sandinista soldiers were in a bad position at the foot of a hill, and we were on top of the hill looking down on them. The battle lasted for twenty-five or thirty minutes. I counted eleven dead government soldiers when it was finished. Not even one of my boys got injured. Afterward, we walked in the direction of Laihn Pihni and the three thousand who had moved out ahead of our position.

The three thousand civilians with Laihn Pihni were far ahead, so we kept on going in their direction. The road, full of mud from the rain, was difficult to travel. I kept thinking of all those old ones and mothers with babies who had passed through that mud, which was often up to our thighs. My heart suffered greatly for them all.

That afternoon at about two-thirty we caught up to some of the people. They were muddied up like we were. There was a nice little river in that place, and we had just started to bathe ourselves when a big group of Sandinistas attacked us. Some of the civilians got injured, so we retreated into the bush, carrying the wounded along with us. By four-thirty in the afternoon it was already dark in that jungle. We decided to sleep where we were, about two hundred yards off the road.

I walked about to check on the Indian people and found many to be sick and injured. Some had been shot badly. Others had injuries from stumbling and falling. I judged the situation to be critical and began to make plans for carrying the sick and injured the remaining distance to Honduras.

Ahead of us was swamp and more mud. Behind us was the enemy. It would not be easy to carry all those people to safety, but that was the problem I had to consider. We would have to support the sick and the wounded, fight the Sandinistas, and protect the bishop and priest. And because the road was very bad and muddy, we would have to sink right down to our shanks to pass through all of it. It was a big problem I contemplated as I walked among those brave Indian people on the night of December 20, 1983.

That night not one of the boys wanted to stand watch because they were all so tired. I told them that a real man cannot be tired. A real man must try to hold up. I was really more tired than they and my bad leg was full of pain, but I took the watch duty. I remembered how grandfather Kleofas had lied to me when he said, "I'm sure I did shoot that deer," and I realized that sometimes a real man, a leader, must make a lie to those who look up to him so that they can have hope and strength in a critical situation. That is why I took watch duty and pretended my strength was still present.

Later one of the boys came to relieve me, but before I could make my hammock ready I heard some strange noises. I told my tired guerrilla boys to get ready because our enemy had caught up to us. There was a brief exchange of gunfire, then the soldiers retreated. We had followed them for about an hour when one boy said, "It is impossible for us to follow them anymore. We'd better go on to rest ourselves."

When we got back to the camp I began to think about how I would manage my Indian people who were sick and injured. It seemed like a bigger problem than ever.

I took my hammock deep into the bush away from the others and tied it to a big ceiba tree. I knew that tree had lots of secrets that I wanted it to give to me. I tied my hammock high on the tree because I knew that snakes would like to sleep with me on such a cold night.

In such jungles, there are many big she-serpents. They like to come to where the warmth is on a cool night, just like a lady coming to lie down in bed close to my side when the night air is cool. The serpent was a clever animal in the Garden of Eden. She is wise and intelligent. Maybe that is the reason why she treats us guerrilla boys in a nice way. She never harms us in that big bush, but just likes to sleep down close with us in our hammocks to stay warm.

Under the sacred tree I considered my problems one by one. I was provoking that tree to give me its secrets, but that great ceiba never did answer my questions, and I fell asleep with many troubles on my soul.

I had a strange dream under that tree. I dreamt that a big black dog was under my hammock. The dog spoke to me about someone. The message was unclear. He entreated me to go with him to see this person. So in my dream I got up from my hammock and followed the dog into the jungle. All night, in my dream, I walked and walked after the big black dog, but the journey seemed to be without reward. When I awoke, I thought to myself, "Well, I have walked all night after that dog and now I am more tired than when I fell asleep."

I did not eat that morning. Instead, I walked through the camp checking on the civilian people, giving them words of encouragement, and making arrangements for carrying the sick and wounded. One family was greatly disturbed because the grandmother, ninety years old, was missing. They told me that she had lain down with them to sleep, but when the morning came she was not there. They could not understand it, because she was weak and sick with arthritis, so how could she have walked away so far? She was not to be found any-where.

The tree had not kept its secrets from me! I felt happy in my heart. How mysterious! If the black dog had not shown me where the old woman was, we would have left her to die there in the jungle, because we did not have the time or the patience to look around the whole area one or two days. But my dream had foretold this event, and the dog had led me along a way and had given me my instructions. I do not know if it was my luck or the old woman's luck, because if we had searched a long time for a human being in that jungle, we would have lost a lot of time. Maybe the enemy would have surprised us, and maybe we would have used up all our ammunition. Also, we did not have food for an extra day. Those were many of the problems I did not have to consider because the tree had considered them for me and had sent the dog into my dream to show me the way. I went into that great jungle and saw with my own eyes the path I had traveled in my dream with the black dog, and I found that dear old one.

In this world many strange things happen that are hard to believe or explain. But we who have been in the jungle for so long—sometimes lost or without food or water—do know that God cares for us and helps us with our troubles in certain secret ways.

On December 21 Honduras was still two days away. It was a huge problem moving three thousand people of all qualities and ages to another country. To be their leader was one heavy responsibility. I remember that I often thought about that time when Moses led the children of Israel to the mountain, because it seemed to me that I was in a similar position.

Moses had a right to get mad, to get discouraged, to get all kinds of bad feelings, because some people are ignorant and unwilling to do what is morally correct. Moses had a right to get mad at Jehovah, who demanded so much of him. That Moses traveled with his people for forty years through mountains and through desert to get to the promised land, so he had a right to be vexed. I, Ráfaga, like Moses when he crossed the Red Sea, had a problem every minute in getting down to the Río Coco. Getting those three thousand Indians and those religious people across that river was all that was on my mind. I knew full well that if I could get them there, that would be my salvation and their salvation as well. It was the same way when Moses was leading the children of Israel from Egypt toward the Promised Land. Just as Pharaoh's gang had followed and harassed the children of Israel all the way to the Red Sea, so did those Sandinista soldiers pursue us, to capture or to kill us, all the way to the Río Coco. Pharaoh's soldiers could travel only on land, but those soldiers of the Sandinistas would hit us from the air with their bombs, from the trees with their bullets, and from the rivers with their gunboats. I believe it was more dangerous for us than for the children of Israel.

The spirit of God was along with the children of Israel because Jehovah spoke directly to Moses. The spirit of God must have been along with the Indians of Francia Sirpe, also, because God did cast the ways and the actions of Moses into the mind and soul of Ráfaga.

I frequently checked on Bishop Schlaefer because that big man was having a hard time walking in his tennis shoes. He told me, "I could not abandon my people. With the time and strength God will give me, I will be willing to travel with you all to the very last minute when we come to the end of the mission."

Four days into the mission, we heard a report on Radio Sandino that "the Contras have kidnapped and killed Bishop Salvador Schlaefer." That was, of course, a lie, but that was what the Sandinistas were broadcasting to the Nicaraguan people.

The government forces had our position marked exactly. Their soldiers were attacking us on every side and from the air above. I needed God's help at every moment. In those moments following a direct strike by the Sandinista forces, I always thanked God for our lives and begged His intervention in our behalf.

I remembered how much the bishop wanted to finish the mission with his people, so I always had him close to me. I was guarding his life so no harm would come to him. The bishop kept praying for us, and for a successful journey to Honduras.

On Radio Sandino we heard them say that the bishop's body had been found. I knew full well what the government was trying to do to us. I knew that the government soldiers would not back off until they had killed the bishop, so that the evil deed would be blamed on us. Soon after we had heard that lie on the radio, I received a radio message from Steadman Fagoth, who was awaiting our arrival on the Honduran side of the Río Coco. Fagoth sounded hot mad, because he too had heard the Sandino report of the bishop's death. Fagoth yelled through the radio, "Is it really true that you killed the bishop?" I said to Fagoth, "Why? Why should I do that?" Fagoth replied, "The whole world is alarmed by the news that you have killed the bishop!" I answered, "The bishop is along with us and he is still alive. Just wait awhile and I'll put him on to talk with you." Fagoth spoke nervously "OK! All right! All right! I'll wait. I will be very glad to speak to the bishop because the American ambassador is right here with me, and if it turns out to be true that you have killed Bishop Schlaefer, then we Contras* are all finished!" I told Fagoth, "I know that! But the bishop is still alive and here with us!"

It was really true that the Sandinista government wanted the bishop dead. Their troops were pounding us from the front and from the back, and from the air they were bombing us. I knew full well that when the Sandinistas intercepted the radio conversation between Fagoth and me they would know of the bishop's well-being, and now they would want more than ever to have him dead, so their version of the story would be believed. The enemy was very, very smart.

I was feeling like it was Jehovah from above who was speaking to me in a spiritual way, just like He had spoken to Moses.

---

*This was Fagoth's designation for the troops. Ráfaga always called them Indian revolutionaries to avoid any confusion with former members of Somoza's National Guard.

That moment—I had to do it quickly—I sent a radio message over to Fagoth that I knew would be heard by the Sandinistas and by the whole world. I wrote the message, which the bishop read into the radio: "I, Salvador Schlaefer, am still alive. If something happens to me, it will be the Sandinista government that has killed me." As the bishop was reading these words into the radio to Fagoth, there was a large group of government reinforcements attacking us from behind. Also, the Sandinista air force was bombing us, and some Sandinista gunboats in the river ahead had prevented our progress. The bishop knew how critical the situation was, so he even bade farewell to his mother over the radio. It was twelve o'clock noon. For a full hour bullets and bombs rained down on us as we tried to protect ourselves.

At one o'clock the bombs quit coming and the guns stopped shooting.

I believe that because the bishop had spoken through the radio with his own voice, heavy pressure from another country must have been put on the Sandinista government to cease firing so that the life of Salvador Schlaefer would be spared. The bishop's voice notified the whole world of the truth, and it was a great event for all the world to know that the bishop was alive. Fagoth told us through the radio that they were receiving messages from all over the world, including from the Vatican, stating their thankfulness for the life of the bishop.

Even though the bullets and bombs had stopped coming at us, there were many problems yet to be faced. I told Fagoth that the bishop and the three thousand civilians were tired and could not walk very well. I told him that we had many wounded and sick ones to carry on our backs and that we were nearly out of food. I asked Fagoth to try to send reinforcements to protect us and some food for the multitude. Fagoth said he would send food, cooks, and a big group of reinforcements led by Comandante Shang. Fagoth also claimed that he would come, himself, to meet us. So we began to travel on toward Honduras.

The bishop never did lose his good humor. He was calm, but he was also tired and slow in his walking because of the great weight pressing down on his swollen and hurt feet. I gave the order to the religious people that they could walk for a half hour, then rest five minutes, then walk another half hour, and so on.

I gave that order on December 21, 1983. I spoke words of encouragement to the boys, who were walking all around the religious people, guarding them. I often spoke with the bishop so he would not feel sad or discouraged. Periodically I would walk back to check on his progress and always found him resting himself just a few feet past the place where I had last seen him. That happened so many times that I reminded him, "I ordered you all to walk for a half hour, then rest five minutes!" I had to be tough on those religious people, but at the same time I showed them my respect. The bishop said to me, "Yes, you gave us orders to walk like that, but I am sorry, we must reverse it or we cannot make it to Honduras. We must walk five minutes then rest for thirty." There was a lot of kidding between us despite our great problems.

There were still many difficulties ahead of us. There were great mountains to climb, and it was steep coming back down. In that kind of country it is easy to fall or get hurt. We had to calculate exactly how and where to put each footstep, because once a slip was made, that person would go straight to the bottom. We had to walk much of the way holding on to the one ahead of us and to ropes we had stretched between us. When there was a river to cross, we would tie a rope to the other side and let the people hold the rope to help them to pull themselves across the water. With all of the wounded and sick ones we had to carry, those ropes helped us plenty.

We guerrilla boys and the civilians managed those problems fairly well because we had always traveled in that kind of wilderness; the bishop and the priest, however, had a much more difficult journey. We Miskito, Sumo, and Rama people have natural training in passing through mountain and through sea. Still, with all of that training, some of the Indians lost their lives.

A few minutes after one o'clock we received a radio message from Fagoth that reinforcements were on their way to meet us. We kept to our course. Later our MISURA scouts came back to me with the information that we were nearing the Río Coco, so we stopped in a little Indian village, where we slaughtered the remaining three cows, cooked the meat, and divided it among the guerrilla boys and the civilians. There we passed the night.

I ordered a few boys to stand guard around the bishop, and we took turns standing watch through the night. I passed that night very close to the religious people. We awakened the morning of December 22 to find that all were OK, so we began to march on toward the Río Coco. Each comandante—Laihn Pihni, Papaya, Mario, and I—had a contingent of the three thousand in our charge. Father Wendelin Shafer asked me how many hours it would be until we reached the Río Coco, and I told him that according to our intelligence report it would be about three hours of walking yet. After three hours had passed, Father Shafer asked me, "Why aren't we at the Río Coco yet?" I explained to the priest that the road was more difficult than we had expected, so it had taken us longer to walk the remaining miles. At about that time I received a radio message from the Honduran side that informed me that our position was still two hours away from Esperanza, the Honduran Indian village where we were to bring the people, and that a reinforcement group of seventy men were traveling to meet us along with Steadman Fagoth. We were also told that many newspaper reporters from Honduras and from all over the world were waiting in Esperanza for our arrival. Every minute of that final part of our journey, Steadman Fagoth was talking to me on the radio, giving me moral support and encouraging me and Laihn Pihni to bring those people over as safely as possible.

That Laihn Pihni was a very brave fellow who had a lot of experience in guerrilla warfare. He had many qualities of a good leader and knew exactly how to handle the civilians who were under his charge. Laihn Pihni, whose home was on the Río Coco, was Steadman Fagoth's number-one friend and received much money from Fagoth. Often he would argue with his Miskito boys and with the other comandantes, but he had many good qualities, much experience in fighting, and had led many successful missions. For those reasons I respected him, and we worked together well on Mission Alpha Uno.

When my group was notified that we still had two hours of walking left before reaching the Río Coco, we were also informed that Laihn Pihni's group was, in fact, already at the river. It was about then that Bishop Schlaefer and Father Wendelin Shafer quit walking because they were really tired and sore. We put him and the priest into hammocks, then we took turns carrying those two religious fellows the rest of the way. I told the bishop that Laihn Pihni's group had already made it down to the Río Coco and that we were going to make it also. We continued on.

I was carrying a young girl called Francisca Davis and the boys were carrying the bishop and the priest in hammocks when Steadman Fagoth met up with us in the road about one hour before we were to reach the river. Immediately, Fagoth went to the bishop to see if he was all right. He gave the religious people tangerines and coffee. After Father Wendelin Shafer ate the fruit, he vomited up everything he had eaten.*

Fagoth became more nervous and discouraged, fearing those men would not survive the remainder of the journey. When Steadman saw how very ill and tired all of us were and how each was carrying another, he asked me, "How in God's name did you travel from Francia Sirpe to this place without getting all of yourselves killed?" I, Ráfaga, replied, "We had to fight like a lion! We had a great and powerful enemy."

Within two hours we reached the Río Coco, where I saw that many of our Indian people had already gone over to the Honduran side. Many Honduran helicopters were in the air. I ordered all of the Indians in my charge to start across the river while I stayed on the Nicaraguan side. I waited and watched as the very last man came out of the river safely on the other side,

---

*Ráfaga did not know at the time that Father Shafer had had heart bypass surgery only one month before. He was vomiting at night and had to have glucose (letter from Bishop Schlaefer to J. K. Wilson, June 24, 1988).

then, like a captain of a ship, I went across last. But before I swam that last distance to liberty, I knelt down on the bank of the Río Coco and there I praised God and thanked Him for staying with us through our perilous journey.

Once on the Honduran side, I felt like a heavy burden had been lifted off of me. As I walked into Esperanza I saw that they had lots of food prepared for the three thousand people we had carried over. Indian musicians were singing Miskito songs to honor us. The newspaper reporters asked me plenty of questions about how we had made that journey. I spoke to representatives from *Newsweek*, the *Washington Post*, the *New York Times*, United Press International, among others. There were newsmen from Europe and Central and South America as well.

I remember that Francisco Baker, the Miskito missionary who had traveled with us, worked a lot when he got to Esperanza. He was one happy fellow, and as he began to serve food to the Indian people he thanked the Lord for bringing us safely to the land of liberty. The MISURA big leaders made speeches of welcome in our honor. While that was happening, a Honduran helicopter picked up the bishop and the other religious people and took them to Tegucigalpa.

That was a big fiesta on that night of December 22, 1983. Steadman Fagoth rejoiced with me, served me food, and made a nice speech in my honor. I had never before seen Fagoth feeling in this nice way about me, and that pleased me, because Fagoth knew full well that I had always opposed his ways, his actions, his bad treatment of the boys, and his opportunistic selfishness.

Only one month earlier, in November 1983, Fagoth had thrown me in jail in Honduras because I had spoken out for the benefit of my boys, demanding that he treat them better. I knew that Fagoth had received millions of dollars from the CIA. (At a future time we learned that he had received $3 million on one occasion and $5 million on another.) Also, I knew that a well-known North American general sent Fagoth many dollars to be used for supplies, but we never saw those supplies.

When I spoke out about that bad treatment, Fagoth had thrown me in jail. But on this night Steadman Fagoth saluted me many times and hugged me twice.

When night came down on us, Steadman began to sing the Miskito song "Tininiska," which tells of a pretty hummingbird. He also sang "Sirpiki-Mairin," which tells about all the pretty young girls. The third song he sang, "Pura Payaska Balka Anira Wamaki," tells about the time when lonesome death is coming and the breath of the Miskito boy is leaving: where will he spend eternity? The fourth, and last, song he sang in our honor was "Luniku Mairinka." which speaks about a young high-sporting man who loves many pretty girls.

Yes, that night Steadman sang and danced until midnight because he was so glad that I, Ráfaga, and Laihn Pihni, along with all of the guerrilla boys, had brought those three thousand Indians, two missionaries, a priest, and Bishop Salvador Schlaefer safely from Francia Sirpe over to Honduras. Mission Alpha Uno had been accomplished.

Nine / Matlalkahbipurayohpa

MISURA Lost/
KISAN Found

That Alpha Uno mission was political work. It was not the first mission of that kind. In mid-1983 another comandante had carried Miskito people from Santa Clara to Honduras. Also, a similar mission, led by Comandante Sutum, had taken the Indians from Slimalia over to the Honduran side.

Just a few days before Alpha Uno began, the Sandinistas had released 307 Miskitos from the jail called Zona Franca. Twenty of those boys joined mission Alpha Uno because they wanted to give their testimony to the news reporters in Honduras about the way they had been mistreated in the Zona Franca jail and to proclaim their opposition to the Nicaraguan government. They wanted the whole world to know what that government was doing to our people.

We, the MISURA comandantes, never forced the people to go over to Honduras. Those who did not want to go never left. All who went went voluntarily. I never forced anyone to go, but I did encourage them to make the journey, and I promised them that they would live better and have all their needs met in Honduras. I promised them that they would have a house, a garden, and freedom to move about because my commander, Steadman Fagoth, had given me this promise for our people, and I believed those promises.

I remember that day when we were getting the people ready to come out of Francia Sirpe, I saw foot-operated sewing machines, one-hundred-pound sacks of beans and rice, a pretty little schoolhouse with plenty of teachers, and lots of

137

pretty good houses, which the Sandinista government built for them. They also had a nice commissary full of goods: machetes, files, and many other things to use for farming. In Francia Sirpe they had a bean plantation that had grown very fine. It was just the time to harvest the crop when we took the people out of their community. Also, there were cows of many breeds—plenty of pigs and chickens, too. All of that they had in their little village.

A few days after our arrival at Esperanza, Honduras, the Indian people from Francia Sirpe were carried to different places—Mocoron, RusRus, Tapamlaya—where they were to be living in that country. During the first weeks of January 1984 I went to each of those places to visit the Indians whom I had carried over because I wanted to see for myself how they were living in this country. What I saw caused me to be very sad. Not even one pound of salt had been given to them.

Fagoth knew that those people had been abandoned and had given them nothing. I remembered their pretty little village of Francia Sirpe, where they had everything nice, and how I had promised, "You will be having it better in Honduras than you are having in Nicaragua." I felt sad and discouraged because my words had been of no value. I cried in my heart for my Indian people.

In February, after I had seen the conditions of the Miskitos in the Honduran refugee camps, I went to Fagoth to tell him that I did not like the way he was treating our people. We had a row and argued very heavily. Fagoth kept saying that he wanted me to lead another political mission like Alpha Uno, but I swore to him, "I will never come back to do that kind of mission to carry my people from their country to another man's country!"

I left for Puerto Lempira, Honduras, and Fagoth followed me to that place and again he asked me to make another mission—Alpha Dos. I told him "No! I will not make another mission of that sort!" Then Fagoth went to the Honduran government and told them lies about me. On February 16, 1984, the Honduran military picked me up and threw me in jail. I was in jail only one day because the Honduran military realized that Fagoth was talking bullshit. Immediately they let me out and gave me my liberty.

The moment I was put in jail, nearly all of the Miskito boys rebelled against Fagoth. Our dislike for that bad fellow grew so big that we decided to organize a meeting to expel him. Brooklyn Rivera was the Miskito leader on the southern front, in Costa Rica, and Wycliffe Diego was second officer under Fagoth on the northern front, in Honduras. We wanted to kick Fagoth out and replace him with Brooklyn, who was our first choice, or with our second choice, Diego.

In that meeting, Steadman Fagoth got only twenty boys to back him. He paid them money to speak in his behalf. But too many of the guerrilla boys were opposed to Fagoth, so we expelled him. He left for his house at RusRus, about three miles away. We used to call that house the "White House" because everything that was happening in the White House in Washington, D.C., was the same thing that was happening in that house of Fagoth's at RusRus.

During the months that followed that first meeting, I visited many clandestine MISURA bases. Fagoth had no real power, and any support that he did have among the Indian fighters quickly diminished. His only visible support was from the twenty or so boys to whom he paid three hundred to five hundred lempiras to guard him and accompany him as he would travel about from base to base behaving as though he were still in command. But in fact, no one took direct orders from him. All of the Miskito fighters took their orders from Fagoth's second officer, Wycliffe Diego, who was then functioning as our unofficial leader. For one full year, that is how the situation continued for us who were based in Honduras.

In March 1985 we had another meeting with the Indian fighters. This meeting was held at the base we called Miskut. Fagoth came to that meeting with his bodyguards, and some of those paid guards stood up in the meeting to speak in his behalf. But the boys were not convinced and voted for Wycliffe Diego to be made the unofficial leader of MISURA. Fagoth tried to ruin the meeting and disrupt the proceedings in every way he could find, but none of his actions brought him any support.

His behavior only turned more of the boys against him, and when the meeting was finished, Fagoth knew that he had no respect from the Miskito fighters.*

After that second meeting Fagoth became less and less visible, then in May or June 1985 we heard that he had gone to Miami Beach to raise some big money for himself. I suspected that it was his intention to return to Honduras to try to fool the boys again. And so it was that he returned in August 1985.

On August 10, 1985, Fagoth and a group of paid fighters launched an attack on the Miskito base at RusRus. They made a direct attack on the hospital there, which the boys were guarding and where many Miskito fighters were hospitalized with injuries sustained in the revolution. The director of that hospital was a man named Chino Solomon. Fagoth captured Chino and seven Indian fighters, then tried to burn the buildings, which were made of palm and wood. Inside the hospital were many Miskito boys who could not run or defend themselves, and it was an evil thing that Fagoth tried to do to them who were inside the buildings. It was a miracle that the hospital did not burn.

Fagoth then went with his bodyguards to the next Indian base, called CIM. There he fought against the Miskito fighters, capturing many and taking their weapons. After finishing the fight at CIM, he went on to Miskut, where I was, and it was there that Fagoth's reign of terror came to an end.

Based at Miskut were 120 or so warriors led by the comandantes Ráfaga, Antonio Talavera (Mamo), Rufus—that man who always wanted to run away—Sutum, Guillermo Recta, "Cara Mala" (Bad Face), and "Cinco Huesos" (Five Bones). For thirty minutes or so we gave Fagoth and his twenty-five boys one very hot fight. There were many opportunities to kill him, but it was not our intention to kill him—only to stop him and put an end to the bad things he was doing. We shot just close enough to him to frighten him. When Fagoth realized that he was not going to take Miskut the way he had taken

*In April 1985 MISURA agreed to a ceasefire with the Nicaraguan government.

RusRus and CIM, he yelled out, "Don't kill me! Have you forgotten that I am your leader? Give me some water and your pardon." He gave himself over to us, admitting his defeat, and I said to him face to face, "You are not our leader. We have no leader who is a murderer like you."

We took Fagoth and his guards as our prisoners, then tied Fagoth to a big pine tree that was there. All day in the hot sun we left him tied to that tree. Some of the boys wanted to kill him, and I had to talk fast so they would not. "It is not right for you to take a man who has given himself up and just kill him like that. If you all disobey my order, it will be a cowardly action." My boys said, "If we can't kill him then we are going to take off all his hair and leave him with a bald head!" Not even for that did I give my permission. When a man is tired and gives himself up in defeat, it is not right to do anything so cowardly.

It was very cold there in the night and very hot in the day, so I just left Steadman fastened to that tree one day and one night for his punishment. We also tied up the guards who were with him and left them all day and all night for the mosquitoes and the flies to feast upon. The following day I notified the Fifth Honduran Military Base of the situation, and they sent a group of soldiers to Miskut to remove Fagoth to jail for his own safety because the boys wanted to kill him. The Honduran soldiers also took eight of Fagoth's top guards. The other twelve we kept as prisoners in our Miskut base. We punished them with hard work and shaved their heads.

Now we began to organize a big meeting, a big assembly that Fagoth could not humbug or black up. All the big leaders— Wycliffe Diego, Alejos Tiofelo, and Roger German—were in the Honduran capitol of Tegucigalpa when we started to organize that big meeting, and I was in the Miskut guerrilla base. We, the Indian fighters, wanted Brooklyn Rivera to come present himself to that assembly because we believed that he was the best leader and that he cared more for the lives of the fighters and for the civilians, as well. Brooklyn was wiser than all of those big leaders in Honduras.

Brooklyn never came to that assembly. Those big leaders in Honduras blocked him from coming, we believe. But many of

Brooklyn's gang who were in Yulo and in Sandy Bay and other places from the bush came to be with us at that great meeting in Miskut.

Miskito women and men living in Honduras, together with Miskitos from Nicaragua, gathered in our Miskut base to begin the assembly on August 25, 1985. Also present were North American newspapermen and other members of the international press. Everyone present totaled about two thousand. Fagoth begged to be pardoned so he could come to that assembly, but we told him no.

We felt that during all those years Fagoth had received money from the U.S. government, he had only helped his family and himself. In 1984 and 1985 he received $10 million of the $110 million appropriated by the U.S. Congress for the counterrevolution. Those who were fighting in the bush did not receive the clothes, food, and weapons they were supposed to. He had moved most of his family out of Nicaragua to Miami Beach and to Los Angeles. His mother's and his wife's families and his cousins were all, by then, living in the United States, and we believed that was where the money was going.

Brooklyn's mother was still living in Sandy Bay. That was one very poor lady. Maybe poorer than my own mother. Also, one of his brothers was a guerrilla fighter and another of his brothers had died fighting in the bush. Fagoth had given one of his brothers a big position administering the money that was coming from the U.S. government. That brother of Fagoth's never went to the front to fight the war. These are some of the reasons why we had more confidence in Brooklyn and more respect for him. That is why we wanted Brooklyn to take responsibility for all of the Indian fighters in Honduras, as well as for those in Costa Rica. It had not been Brooklyn's style to have Miskito people murdered like Fagoth had done.

Two of Brooklyn's comandantes came to our meeting at Miskut: Comandante Simfuryano Night ("Kusuwa," Turtle) and Comandante Kenneth Bushy ("Kakamuk," Iguana). Those boys were intelligent and true to their words. In the assembly Diego, Tiofelo, and German had one big debate with those two boys, who were supporting their commander. Kakamuk and

Kusuwa were presenting some points about Brooklyn's qualities as a leader and about Brooklyn's hopes for his people
when the big leaders from Tegucigalpa began to argue with
them. It was clear to all of us that Brooklyn's understanding of
our problems and of the problems of the Miskito nation was
in agreement with that of the Indian fighters.

On the following day, August 26, we began to think about
changing the name of our fighting organization. It was our
determination to completely reorganize the structure of the
leadership and to choose a new name. There was a great
debate about these topics, and at last it came out that we would
call ourselves KISAN. MISURA was lost. KISAN signified "Kosta
atlantica Indians ka nani Sut Aslatakan Nicaragauza,"; in English: Atlantic Coast Indians united in Nicaragua.

Another important outcome of this meeting was a commitment to turn away from mistreating Indian people in the villages
of Nicaragua and in the refugee camps of Honduras. There
were many Indian civilians at the meeting who made their
complaints known to us about how they had been treated by
MISURA. Everyone who wanted to speak about their complaint
was allowed to speak.

Some of the civilians reported that many of the guerrilla boys
had come into their Indian villages and had mistreated them.
And so it was that we all agreed together, with the guerrilla
boys and with the civilians, that this kind of treatment would
not be condoned by KISAN.

On August 27 we elected Wycliffe Diego to be our leader.
Diego was not our first choice, but he was the best of those
leaders who were willing to take responsibility for KISAN's
leadership. Brooklyn did not present himself, and Fagoth was
not wanted by anyone; therefore, we had to choose another.
When we restructured the organization, we put at the top a
consejo de ancianos, a council of "old heads" or advisors.
This was our way of guaranteeing that the leader would abide
by the general principles of KISAN. Should he change his
thinking or act badly toward the Indian fighters or the Indian
civilians, then the council had the power to remove him. All of
these arrangements were agreed upon by everyone present,

Organizational Structure of KISAN

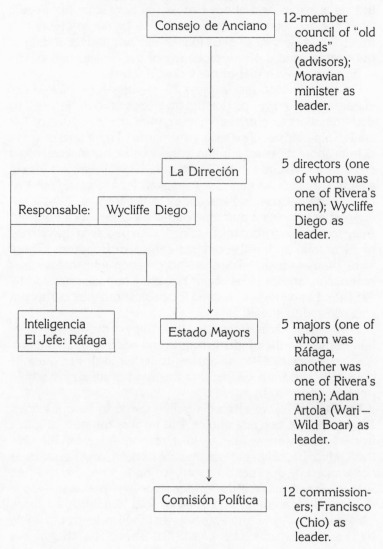

Consejo de Anciano — 12-member council of "old heads" (advisors); Moravian minister as leader.

La Dirreción — 5 directors (one of whom was one of Rivera's men); Wycliffe Diego as leader.

Responsable: Wycliffe Diego

Inteligencia El Jefe: Ráfaga

Estado Mayors — 5 majors (one of whom was Ráfaga, another was one of Rivera's men); Adan Artola (Wari — Wild Boar) as leader.

Comisión Política — 12 commissioners; Francisco (Chio) as leader.

including Diego. In the assembly, right in front of everyone present, the council explained this to Diego and Diego agreed. Every idea was right out in the open. There were no secrets, and everyone, including the leaders, fully understood what was to be expected from KISAN. There was much emphasis placed on the Comisión Política, so that the work of KISAN could concentrate much more on political matters in addition to the military responsibilities. And this was to be at the direction of the Comisión Política and not of the CIA. The Estado Mayors were the military leaders; one comandante called "Wari" (Wild Boar), whose real name was Adan Artola, was put at the head of that group. I was elected chief of intelligence and was also a member of Estado Mayors.

On August 28 the assembly came to an end. We had finished our work. That same day Fagoth was thrown out of the country.

LIBRO UNICO

Libro Unico was the secret book of MISURA. In it were written various delicate secrets to which nobody had access other than the chief of intelligence and four or five of the organization's top leaders. An Indian, Mario Cordoba, who was the outgoing chief of intelligence, delivered all the documents of his intelligence section to me in August 1985 when MISURA became KISAN. These secrets were not known by the line commanders, those who were fighting. When I received these documents I started to read them, and more than anything I focused on the contents of *Libro Unico*. It contains the secrets of the MISURA organization during the time Steadman Fagoth was in charge.

The book revealed that MISURA had been receiving money, arms, and directions from the CIA. It also recorded the alliance between MISURA and the former National Guard officers of Somoza (the Contras). In 1982 MISURA received money and excellent weapons such as American M16s, Argentine FALs, Chinese AK-47s, Czechoslovakian AK-45s, M79 grenade launchers, mortars, and machine guns, among others. Many of these weapons were delivered by Fagoth to the Honduran military officers based close to the Atlantic Coast, especially the M16s and FALs. In exchange, he received M1 carbines (from World War II, as I understand it). There were only enough weapons for eighteen hundred of our ten thousand men, so we had to take turns going on missions. The ones who remained in camp went fishing, found jobs, or got married in Honduras. When we encountered the well-equipped Sandinistas on the battlefield, we quickly realized that the carbines were useless for a force that was trying to win a war. The weapons would literally fall apart in our hands as we fought. I interpret Fagoth's shameful and traitorous act as the cause of the deaths of many of my Indian brothers.

Similarly, the money he received from the CIA was divided up among the four or five leaders as a monthly salary. Some received 800 lempiras (266 U.S. dollars in 1984), others 1,000. We were not aware of this at all.

Regarding the alliance with the ex-officers of Somoza's National Guard, I remember that there were a few of them among us as advisors from 1982 to 1984, but we were unaware of the extent of the accords and the financial arrangements. Early on, there was a large group of advisors who were paid to help train us, about twelve of them. It was not pleasant having them around. We protested and most of them left, but a few of them stayed—the ones nicknamed "Mercenary," "79," and "45." These men were experts with weapons and advised us well. They also treated us well, because they knew that one false step would bring us to oppose them.

I never planned to keep these matters secret. For me, they were shameful things that had to come to light. I let most of the line commanders know about these things. They deserved to know what their top MISURA leaders had been doing. Those leaders had never come into Nicaragua to fight. They had never confronted the enemy. They just stayed in Honduras, not even in the clandestine bases, but in the capital city, Tegucigalpa, in an office from which they conducted their political work. They never experienced the blows and sufferings of the battlefield and the jungle. They never felt the love that one guerrillero has for another when he says, "compañero." It is a greater love than one has for one's own blood brother. If you are hungry, the compañero shares food with you. If you are sick, he stays to watch over you. If a compañero has a cigarette, it belongs to the whole group. I remember many times when we shared a cigarette among forty men. All we could really do was smell the smoke, not even inhale. But those men in the office, when they arrived at our camps, they dressed up in military uniforms and boots and took pictures of themselves carrying weapons to make the claim that they were fighters. When my compañeros heard these secrets and became aware that they had been fighting a prolonged guerrilla war for Washington and were not supposed to win, at least not for twenty years, like it took the Sandinistas, they were furious.

After breaking this news to them, we had long discussions in which I tried to explain to them that the Sandinistas had accomplished their revolution as much through words and beautiful songs of protest as on the battlefield. They won through what we call the war of blah-blah-blah. And they had a country of 2.5 million or more united behind them when they triumphed. In contrast, there are only 200,000 Miskitos, and they are divided. Most of the teachers and workers, our best-trained people, had become Sandinistas. We who were in exile numbered about ten thousand men in 1982, but we were poorly equipped to fight, and many of our boys were so young that they did not understand what they were fighting for. We hardly had a chance, especially not in prolonged guerrilla warfare.

Still, men from the CIA would come to talk to us about the dangers of Sandinista expansionism and the threat to the interests of the United States. They never spoke to us about the rights of the Nicaraguan Indians or of any Central American Indians. There was apparently no plan for the future government of the Atlantic Coast if we should win. We did not matter to them. We were just meat to them, nothing more.

The Splitting of KISAN

All these realizations about the corruption of our leaders moved us toward dialogue with the Sandinistas. We knew that we would not get 100 percent of what we wanted from them, but at least we could gain some of our lost rights through a process of dialogue. There was no hope of getting anything through further fighting under the conditions that the United States and our Miskito leaders had arranged.

CONVERSION IN SAUPUKA

Immediately after the Miskut assembly, we began to organize missions to Nicaragua so we could inform the Indian people living and fighting there about the new organization KISAN. I was elected to lead a political mission into Nicaragua to deliver this message and to gather information about the Sandinista bases there.

In September 1985 I left Miskut in a little pickup truck with fifteen guerrilla fighters. Our first stop was at Auka, Honduras, then we passed through Base no. 50. It was at Base no. 50 that I received a radio message from Diego that the enemy was watching us. I sent some of the boys out from that base to see if our enemy was near. They reported that our way was safe to travel on, so we started for Saupuka, Nicaragua, in five little canoes.

Saupuka was one of those little Río Coco villages where the Sandinistas had removed all the people. The people had been sent to an *asientamiento* called Sumobila. For many months

148

no one had been living there in Saupuka. But recently those people had been allowed to return to their village, and about five hundred were living there when we arrived.

As soon as we came into the village, the Indian people gathered together to tell me what had been happening to them at Sumobila and what had been happening to the other Indians living on the Atlantic Coast. I had spent two days in Saupuka when the old heads came to see me, saying there was a large group of Sandinistas very near the community. It was my thinking that the government troops were planning to attack us, so I asked the old heads, "How many arms do you all have here in this little village?" I believed we would have to combine our resources if we were going to fight the Sandinistas. An old head replied, "We don't have anything—we only have one .22 long rifle here. Why do you want to know this?" I said, "If the Sandinistas come to attack, we are going to fight." I saw that these old heads were curiously unafraid, and yet they showed signs of being worried. I, too, was worried for these people because we were just sixteen in number. I asked the boys if they were willing to fight if the Sandinistas attacked us. They said, "Anything you want, we are willing to do."

We began preparations to fight. The Saupuka people came to me saying that these Sandinistas had not come to fight. I asked, "Well, then, what do they want?" But the Saupuka people told me nothing. I sensed that this was a strange situation. Finally, Tejada Salazar, the chief of the old heads, said to me, "My commander, we don't want any more shedding of blood here. That's why I never let you know that I went to meet with the Sandinistas." He told me that he had traveled to the government base at Sisin, near Puerto Cabezas, to ask the Sandinistas to come to Saupuka. Tejada said he had told them, "You must please come to Saupuka to speak to Comandante Ráfaga and try to make peace." That was the reason the soldiers were waiting near the little village. They were waiting for me, Ráfaga.

Then I said, "Get all the people together, the whole town." Everyone came together, and I asked, "What do you want to do here? What is your thinking?" Those Indian people told me they did not want any more shedding of the blood of Indian people and did not want to worry anymore. One woman told me, "Three of my sons have been killed in the fighting, and my grandson is dead because of this war." She was crying. She did not want any more fighting. She said she did not want one more sister or mother or grandmother to shed any more tears for this killing. I told her, "I did not come here to talk to Sandinistas! My mission here is not to speak to or have any argument with the government. But if the people want this to be, then I, Ráfaga, will talk with them."

I had not come to Saupuka to fight or to talk with the Sandinistas. My mission was to find the government military bases, to inform the Indians about KISAN, and to discuss with them what their situation had been at Sumobila. I had wanted to know if they needed any materials, food, tools, and so on, with which to rebuild their lives now that they had returned to their home village. Or, if they were not happy there, I wanted to discover if they would prefer to be in Honduras. These were the real reasons why my boys and I had come to the community.

Tejada Salazar brought a message to me from the soldiers camped near the village. The Sandinistas had invited me to come to the place where they were waiting so we could talk. I told Tejada to return to the camp with this message: "If you want to see me or to speak to me, three of you must come to meet me here in the town schoolhouse. Ráfaga."

On September 13, 1985, three well-armed Sandinistas came to the schoolhouse at Saupuka. Their names were Edgar Sanchez, Benito Torrez, and Francisco Morales. There was great tension in the community. Some of the people thought the government officers were going to use this opportunity to kill me. They told me not to go. But I was not afraid. I wanted to follow through with this meeting to try to attain peace. Kill me or not, I wanted to try because the old heads had advised me in this way.

I asked all the people to go to the school to be witness to this meeting. Then three of my boys and I, all well-armed, went into that place and sat down on a bench facing the three

Sandinistas, who were also sitting on a bench. I believed that Benito was thinking like I was: "If KISAN wants to kill me, then Ráfaga is going to die also." During every moment of the meeting, we were both thinking of this possibility.

Benito told me that he believed Tomás Borge (minister of the interior) and President Daniel Ortega wanted peace on the Atlantic Coast. He said that they recognized that we Indians wanted our rights and that the big commanders in the Nicaraguan government were ready and willing to talk with us, but not with the Hispanic Contras. At that time I had no proof that Benito was speaking for Borge, the minister of the interior. But weeks later I would discover that it had been at Borge's direct order that Benito and the others had come to Saupuka to talk with me.

Initially I responded in this way: "KISAN is an organization with a leader, Wycliffe Diego. If you want to talk to KISAN, it makes no difference who agrees. All the Indians in the Atlantic Coast can agree that this should be so, but only Diego can send someone to talk with you. This is not my mission. I did not come here to have any dialogue with you or anything of the sort. My mission is not for that. I am the chief of intelligence for KISAN, not the head of the organization. If there is a decision to negotiate with the government, it is not my decision to make."

I believed that the people of this one little village wanted someone to negotiate with the government, but I did not know how the people in other villages were thinking. It had been many months since I had been in Nicaragua, so I was curious to know the opinions of the old heads about this war we were fighting. I told the three Sandinistas, "I will have to go to plenty of different villages to talk with my people. If the people agree, like the Saupuka people have, then maybe I will be able to speak to you in a dialogue."

Benito Torrez agreed to provide three trucks to transport us to the other villages, twenty-nine in all, to visit with the old heads and with the people. He guaranteed that no Sandinista soldiers would bother us while we were traveling all around the Atlantic Coast. To fortify this promise, I suggested that Benito travel with me at my side. And so it was that my boys, several old heads, Benito, and some of his soldiers and officers traveled side by side in those three trucks.

I was carrying Benito at my side in the second truck. If the government soldiers wanted to fight me, then the two of us would die together. In the back of our truck were five of my boys and three of Benito's boys. The third truck carried the old heads and three of Benito's officers. The first truck I sent ahead of the rest so they could inform the village of our coming, make preparation for food, and establish the security of the area.

As we bumped along the road, Benito and I had good conversations, just like two Nicaraguans talking. We talked about war not being the way to bring peace. We talked about the many deaths and troubles of our people. Also, we talked about our personal miseries. Benito said, "Ráfaga, I am tired of this war. I have spent three years on this Atlantic Coast side. I want to visit my family on the Pacific side. I want to be living with my children and my wife, but this war will not permit that because I am obliged to work on this side." I told Benito that I had been living many months in the mountains like an animal. I told him about our guerrilla life in the jungle and that we missed our families just like he did.

We visited many Indian villages where we had meetings with the old heads and with the whole town. In the order of our travels, the villages we visited were: Bilwaskarma, Saklin, Wasla, Tuskru-Sirpe, Tuskru-Tara, Bihmuna, Santa Marta, Pahara, Kum, Sisin, Krukira, Auyapihni, Bom-Sirpe, Kambla, Dakura, Sandy Bay, Lidakura, Uskira, Awasyari, Awastara Kahtkah, Wahka-Laya, Rahwa-Unta, Kistawan, Tuapi, Lamlaya, Ninayari, Yulo, and Puerto Cabezas.

While I was in Krukira and in Sandy Bay, I spoke on the radio to Adam Artola, who was commander at our Honduran base called Miskut. I also spoke to Wycliffe Diego. I told them about what was happening, telling them that in every village I was finding that all of the Indians living there wanted peace. I explained to the *cupula* (high command) that the old heads of each village wanted a peace dialogue to begin.

My commanders in Honduras said that were opposed to this proposal. They said that the Indians and the old heads still living in Nicaragua did not understand how the Sandinistas were really thinking and that this kind of dialogue would produce no kind of peace. Diego and Artola said they were going to keep on fighting. I pleaded with them to consider the opinions of our people, especially the thinking of our old heads, but Diego and Artola could not be persuaded. When I told them that I was becoming more and more convinced of the possibilities of a dialogue, they ordered me to return to Honduras immediately.

Up until three months before I was making these visits to the Indian villages, an Indian leader from Yulo named Eduardo Pantin ("Laihn Pauni," Red Lion) had been talking with the government about a dialogue. In June 1985 Laihn Pauni was killed by a bullet from a gun that discharged when it fell from his vest pocket onto the floor of his house where a meeting was in progress. The bullet struck him in the heart. In Yulo there were about two hundred Indian fighters who had been under his command. After the accident an Indian named Comandante Barbon took command of the Yulo boys. But he did not feel that he had the capacity to continue the dialogue with the government as Laihn Pauni had been doing. Also, Comandante Juan Salgado was in Yulo, but like Barbon he was feeling not equal to the task of the dialogue. In Sisin and Bom-Sirpe, comandantes Black Eagle and Tarim were still more interested in fighting than in dialogue; therefore, establishing peace with the government had been slow, even though these comandantes had left MISURA in favor of peace talks.

Many of the Yulo boys wanted a dialogue, but they had no leader capable of the task since the death of Laihn Pauni. When I left Krukira, I had not made a decision whether to stay for the dialogue or to return to Honduras. I was thinking about the possible outcomes of each path. Comandante Tarim gave me twenty of his boys should I need protection traveling back to Honduras. Tarim also had captured seven of Barbon's boys and punished them by shaving their heads. Tarim gave me those seven to take to Honduras, saying, "You had better take them because I will kill them if they stay here." I took the seven and the twenty with me to Sandy Bay, where we were to have another town meeting. In that time I was thinking more of returning to Honduras, but the Moravian minister in Sandy Bay, Nicho, came with a group of Indian people to beg me not to return to the fighting.

Tarim's seven prisoners with the shaved heads pleaded with me to go to their Yulo base to begin a dialogue and to take charge of the fighters there who were hoping for a peace without war. Nicho arranged a memorial service at the Moravian church to honor the boys from Sandy Bay who had died fighting in the war, and he asked me to stand before the congregation to read each dead Indian boy's name. This I agreed to do before returning to Honduras. While I was doing that—reading the list name by name—my thinking and my conscience began to grow toward a decision to stay in my country. When I had finished reading that list of names, some of which were former students of mine, I knew that I was not going to return to more fighting.

Nicho began raising some money in Sandy Bay so we could travel to Puerto Cabezas and talk to the big Sandinista leaders there. I was waiting in Sandy Bay, preparing for a trip to Puerto Cabezas, when Benito sent a radio message to Jose "Chepe" Gonzales, the head Sandinista leader in Puerto Cabezas, to tell him of our plans. Soon after, a helicopter carrying Chepe, Salvador Perez, and Cesar Paris arrived in Sandy Bay. The leaders had come there to talk with me about the prospects of a dialogue. This was in the first week of October 1985. After the meeting the three of them returned to Puerto Cabezas. Then, a second time, those same Sandinista leaders came to Sandy Bay to persuade me to go with them. On that second visit I agreed. So I went to Puerto Cabezas, where we began to talk about the logistics of a dialogue.

NEGOTIATION IN MANAGUA

For four days I was in Puerto Cabezas talking with Chepe and the other big leaders of the Sandinistas when the minister of the interior, Tomás Borge, called on the government radio to speak with Chepe and with me about the possibility of a dialogue for peace.* It was then that I learned of Borge's prior knowledge of what had been happening between me and the government officers since that first meeting in Saupuka. Borge invited me to meet with him in Managua so we could establish the structure of the dialogue and to find out from each other what specific outcomes and guarantees both sides expected.

In October 1985 Chepe and I left for Managua to meet with Borge. With me I took twenty-nine old heads, one from each of the villages I had visited. Initially, we had four meetings with Borge, which were held in a house at Las Colinas. Accompanying Borge were his second officers Rene Vivas and Mario Mejia.

We told Borge that the Atlantic Coast Indians were not satisfied with the situation between themselves and the government and that we would stand ready to fight until it got better. I told the minister that I had been willing to keep on with the fight, but that the old heads were thinking about a dialogue, and out of my respect for them and for all of the Indian boys dead in the war, I was now willing to try to engage in a dialogue with the Sandinista government.

All of us at Las Colinas helped to set the foundation for the dialogue. We agreed that Yulo would be the place where the dialogue would begin. But in order for that to be a reality, several points of agreement had to be established. First, the Indians wanted Yulo to be declared a peace zone 880 miles square. This zone we would defend against all intruders— Sandinistas, Contras, or Indian revolutionaries—who might disturb our territory. We made a bilateral agreement with Borge that we the Indian fighters would not be taking any more guns or bullets from Costa Rica or from Honduras. The government, in turn, promised to give us every kind of military matériel we

---

*In 1984, MISATAN was founded by thirty-three Miskito communities seeking dialogue and peace. In July 1985, the National Autonomy Commission issued a tentative autonomy document for discussion in town and village meetings on the Atlantic Coast. The fact that Ráfaga mentions neither of these merely demonstrates how difficult it was to coordinate the relations of military and political organizations in that period.

should need to defend Yulo. We told Borge that no Sandinista troops must ever try to enter the peace zone and that we would not permit any Contras or Indian revolutionaries to enter either. Yulo was to become a center of dialogue where there would be no warring with weapons. Those who wanted to enter the zone for peaceful reasons would be permitted.

Once the logistics of the dialogue had been established, the bilateral agreement was drawn up:

1. The government would release all Indians held in *asientamientos* and help them to return to their river village homes.
2. As long as the dialogue was engaged by both sides in good faith, no Indian boys would be forced into the Sandinista military.
3. All Indians of the Atlantic Coast could move freely from place to place without need of a *cedula,* a written identification document.
4. The government would give material aid to help rebuild the village houses and buildings destroyed by the war.
5. The government would give financial aid to Indian widows and orphans.
6. Medical assistance would be given free to all Indians in need of attention.
7. Government banks would provide loans to Indians wishing to rebuild their plantations.
8. We must begin to study, together, ways to bring the Atlantic Coast of Nicaragua into an autonomous state.

Borge and we agreed together on these points. Then we began to talk about which political man could lead the Indian people. The twenty-nine old heads met and agreed that Brooklyn Rivera was the only man who had the respect of the people and the education necessary to fill that position properly. And so for the second time in so many months we tried to summon Brooklyn to the aid of the Miskito people.

I called Brooklyn via telephone in San Jose, Costa Rica. The man who received my call was one of Brooklyn's officers, Marcos Huffington. Marcos said, "Brooklyn is not here in the San Jose office." Several times I made the call, and each time I was told, "He is not here." Finally, one of Brooklyn's officers named Uriel Zuniga answered, saying, "Please don't call anymore, because Brooklyn doesn't want to answer you." We then asked Jimmy Webster, a Moravian minister from Krukira and good friend of Brooklyn's, to intervene in our behalf. Jimmy tried several times to speak to Brooklyn after explaining our situation to his officers, but Brooklyn would talk to no one. If Brooklyn had accepted this responsibility at the time, he would now be an established political leader in Nicaragua. But instead today he is a political corpse begging to negotiate with the government.

We were all in agreement that we should not give up on the idea of bringing Brooklyn in as the political liaison between the Indians and the government. We decided on a plan to send me to Mexico to try to establish contact with Brooklyn's officers Kenneth Bushy and Simfuryano Night, who were based in Honduras at the time.

While that plan to contact Bushy and Night was being devised, I returned to the Atlantic Coast to report the outcomes of the dialogue and to attend to my boys in Yulo. At the same time, the Sandinista government sent ten of the Miskito elders who had been with me in Managua to Cuba. They were in Cuba for two weeks observing the outcome of that country's revolutionary process. Many of them were treated for various diseases. One, whose face had been constantly inflamed and infected for many years, was treated in a Cuban hospital and completely cured. All ten of the elders were given physical examinations, and all their dental problems were corrected. The Cuban government took them to different parts of the country to see work centers, sporting centers, development projects, hospitals, and bus and boat factories. For the first time in our history, Miskito elders got to know another country. Many of the elders had never even been to Managua, much less to another country. The ten came back to the Atlantic Coast feeling very happy about their trip. They told me that it was incredible how the Cuban revolution had advanced the country and how greatly they were appreciated by the Cuban officials and the people.

After the elders returned to Nicaragua, Tomás Borge invited me to Managua to discuss how I would try to contact Bushy and Night, who by that time were in Honduras working in the KISAN organization. He proposed that I go to Mexico and try to contact them from there. He also invited me to make a trip to Cuba first. Borge said, "Hey, *hombre,* after so much suffering, you deserve to see those places." When Borge speaks to me, I understand him easily. He knows what guerrilla life is like. So we understand each other well. At first, when he offered me the trip I told him I could not travel there because I had much work to attend to. The dialogue had only recently started, and I was feeling insecure about leaving my troops for so long because I felt they might go back to the mountains to fight. But finally I accepted his invitation, and in late October 1985 I left Managua to travel first to Cuba and then to Mexico.

What I could not have known ahead of time was that two or three days before my arrival in Havana, a hurricane had destroyed electric poles, dikes, and houses. The streets were full of tree limbs, and everyone was busy with the cleanup. Accompanied by two Sandinistas, I arrived at the airport and was received by a diplomatic delegation from the Nicaraguan embassy. They drove me to the Habana Libre Hotel, where my accommodations had been arranged. The two Sandinistas stayed in other quarters, but when the car would come to pick me up to take me around to see the countryside and the different projects, those two Sandinistas were always along with us. They had a lot of money and offered to take me to dances and fine hotels. Many times I was invited to drink good whiskey, but I always declined their invitations.

Like the elders, I was shown many schools, hospitals, and projects that were indeed quite nice. I wanted to see the things that were *not* quite so nice, however, because I believed that what the elders had told me of their trip might not apply to all the Cuban people. The two Sandinistas always showed me beautiful places, abundant fruits, and happy students, reminding me that "someday Nicaragua will be nice like this." But after I returned to the hotel each day, I would walk to various parts of the city and talk with the common people.

One day, I remember, an article about my visit to the country appeared in one of the Havana newspapers. That evening I walked to a park only a block from the hotel. I met a lot of people who had read the article and were anxious to talk to me after I had introduced myself to them. They told me about the other side of life in Cuba. I discovered that not all aspects of life there were as nice as the projects and people to which I had officially been introduced. The men in the park told me that the Cuban peso was officially worth more than the dollar, but everybody wanted dollars because they could not buy certain things without dollars. That political game of overvaluing the peso really shocked me. Those people who do not have dollars go hungry and suffer from desiring things they cannot have. I was troubled by this. Also in the park were long lines of people waiting their turn to buy a bit of ice cream. There were lines everywhere.

On another day the car came to take us to an institute where I saw many students from India, Afghanistan, Africa, and Nicaragua studying various trades and professions. Later that week a boy and a girl whom I had met at the institute came to find me at the hotel and visited with me for about two hours. They wanted me to know that the foreign students such as themselves were provided with good food and lodging, while the Cuban students were given worse provisions. They showed me empty pharmacies, cars falling apart, shortages of milk, and other scarcities. I cannot say whether the motive of the Cuban government is political or humanitarian, but I did see that the Cuban people sacrifice a lot to provide good food and lodging to the foreign students.

During a trip to an agricultural project located in Pinar del Río, I spoke with workers who said they had no milk or meat for their families and sometimes had no rice or beans. I remembered how the Cuban ships had come to the Atlantic Coast every two or three months to bring my people rice, beans, coffee, and milk, and I realized how their farm workers had to go without many basic food items so that people living on the Atlantic Coast of Nicaragua could have a little something to eat. I saw things that my elders had not seen. The reality was that in Cuba there were many poor people. The country was not a total place of glory like my two Sandinista guides told me. I felt grateful to the common people for their sacrifices.

I was in Cuba for eight days and then flew to Mexico City, where I was met at the airport by a gentleman from the Nicaraguan embassy. The two Sandinistas who had accompanied me to Cuba went with me to Mexico; as in Cuba, they stayed elsewhere while I stayed at the Hotel Diplomático.

As Borge and I had planned, I telephoned Joraila Bushy, a Miskito Indian leader who was then living in Tegucigalpa, Honduras, with her American husband, a Baptist missionary. Joraila Bushy was a native of Nicaragua's Atlantic Coast and had left that area following the Triumph of 1979. I had known her during the time when I was based in Honduras, and I knew she was a close friend of Kenneth Bushy and Simfuryano Night, Rivera's boys who had come to our big meeting at Miskut and who by this time were working in Diego's KISAN organization. It was my intention to ask Joraila to tell these two comandantes about the dialogue so the KISAN leadership might begin to have some confidence in what was happening between the Miskito nation and the Sandinista government.

Joraila flew to Mexico City and stayed at the same hotel as I did. We met every day for six continuous days discussing the dialogue and the possible outcomes. The two Sandinistas who had accompanied me to Mexico brought with them videotapes showing the Miskito elders and myself in dialogue with Borge. Joraila saw the videotapes but was not convinced. Her response was guarded. While she expressed much happiness with our engaging in talks with the government, she said that the Sandinistas had never kept their promises. I told her about my experiences with Borge in behalf of our Miskito people and told her that the meetings were conducted in a friendly manner and with mutual respect. I related to her that Borge had told me, "You have every right to claim your Indian rights and to defend your principles because these are your historic possessions." Borge had encouraged me to convey to her his regret about the way the government had treated our people for lack of understanding of the Indian ways, and about the many errors made by the government regarding our Miskito nation. I asked Joraila to consider the possibility of convincing Kenneth Bushy and Simfuryano Night to join me in the dialogue.

When we had finished our discussions, she returned to Honduras with the information I had given her, saying she would consider the situation with sincere hopefulness. And even though I kept a hopeful spirit about the possibility of Bushy and Night joining us, I felt that Joraila had not fully appreciated the goodwill of the government as I had experienced it through Borge. I felt compelled then and now to proclaim my true feelings about Borge. In all of my dealings with him in behalf of my people and on a personal level, he has every time kept his word and demonstrated a genuine desire to understand our problems completely.

I never spoke again with Joraila and do not know whether she conveyed my messages to Bushy and Night. Those two comandantes never did express a desire to join our dialogue. To my knowledge, no real progress resulted from that trip to Mexico. I have wondered how things might have been different had Bushy and Night been convinced to participate with us. That participation might have brought Rivera into a more agreeable position, and our people might not have had to suffer longer without a strong political leader. But this we can never know.

PEACE IN YULO

On November 13, 1985, I returned to Nicaragua from Mexico to visit with my children in Managua for fifteen days. During that visit I met with Borge several times before flying back to the Atlantic Coast. On one of those visits he presented me with a handsome gold and silver pistol. That is the gun I still carry today.

In December I flew to Puerto Cabezas. When I arrived, Chepe Gonzales gave me money to give to the Yulo boys to help them pass the Christmas. He said the Christmas money was a gift from Borge. I took the money to Yulo and divided it among the four hundred boys there, then passed December 24 and 25 with my boys.

The Yulo boys and I agreed that we in the peace zone would be known as KISAN por la Paz (KISAN for Peace). When news of this reached Honduras, Diego began referring to his organization as KISAN por la Guerra (KISAN for War). This seemed to signify the unofficial splitting of KISAN. It was well established by then that part of KISAN was in dialogue in Yulo and another part was making war from Honduras. The Yulo boys elected me to be *el jefe del estado mayors* (chief of all the ranked majors) for KISAN por la Paz. In that role I functioned as the head military defense commander of that peace zone.

The new year of 1986 came, and with its coming I had much work to do. I traveled about to the various villages—Sukatpin, Lapan, Maniwatla, Forty-three, Clima, and Dakban—where the Miskitos were living. Each week more and more Indian fighters would return from Honduras. They would hear about our dialogue for peace in Yulo and would volunteer to be part of KISAN por la Paz. During those visits to the Indian villages, I found many old people, babies, and young fighter boys who were sick and in need of help. As I traveled, I kept a list of the various needs of people, then would present it to Chepe Gonzales in Puerto Cabezas. There were many needs: clothing, food, medical supplies, construction materials, and so forth. The government always kept their part of the bargain, providing me with everything for which I asked. They also sent a doctor and two nurses, who accompanied me to many communities that had had no medical services for years. As soon as these basic needs began to be met, I started looking to the problems of the farming and fishing activities.

Chepe and I went to the Banco Popular de Desarrollo (People's Development Bank) in Puerto Cabezas to talk to them about loans for Indians who wanted to reestablish their plantations or their fishing businesses. That is how the Miskito boys got the money to start to make their farms or to make their fishing boats. They began behaving themselves and working honorably to provide food and fish for their villages.

In May 1986 Wycliffe Diego sent the first group of KISAN por la Guerra fighters to attack us at Yulo. Comandante Ulu (Wasp) and about thirty fighters came to our peace zone to destroy us. We invited them in to have a meeting with us, and in that meeting I told them that if they wanted to fight us, they would have to fight us in another place, that Yulo was a place for talking, not for fighting. The next day Comandante Ulu returned and again I explained our purpose, assuring him that if his intention was to kill us all, we would give him that opportunity, but not in Yulo. After that second meeting, Ulu disappeared. I do not know where he went. Possibly he went back to Honduras to tell Diego what KISAN por la Paz was about.

June 1986 brought another group of Diego's men to kill us in Yulo. Two commanders, Mauricio Isaias and David Clark, came with forty-five fighters. We had been told by Sandy Bay and Tuara people that this group was coming after us to destroy Yulo and to kill Comandante Ráfaga. So before they arrived, I took some of the boys about three miles outside the peace boundary to face the group. When I saw Mauricio's face, I knew it was not looking friendly, not with good intentions. I just treated them well, like a peacemaker, inviting them to come talk with us in Yulo.

Mauricio and David, along with some of their boys, did come with us. I spoke to them about our dialogue with the government, telling them of the many ways we had been working well with Chepe Gonzales and with Borge and how the peace had been kept in Yulo now seven months or more. I explained to them my reasons for quitting the fight and my resentments toward the MISURA and KISAN leadership for its mistreatment of the Indian refugees in Honduras. I was trying to bring them over to our way of working for victory without more shedding of Indian blood. I told them about the old heads' hopes for peace and reminded them that this was our traditional way of living—the way of taking advice from our old chiefs, not from leaders in Honduras who were being advised by CIA or from leaders in Costa Rica who were being advised by North American anthropologists and lawyers. I said to them, "The old race doesn't want any more of this shedding of blood, and we need to cooperate with the old people."

Furthermore, I explained, "If Fagoth and Diego think you

can fight and win, then why have they both carried all of their families to Miami Beach? Why did Steadman buy a big-time house in Florida? Why? That is to show you he had no hope of winning. Use your common sense. They have all of you thinking like fools. Those leaders and their families have been living well off the money that was meant for the poor boys who were fighting and shedding their blood. We are men with enough knowledge and sense who have been to school a little and who have our eyes open enough to know that those leaders are treating us like damn fools."

I believed that if all of the communities of the Atlantic Coast were begging for peace and we guerrilla boys kept fighting, we could have no victory. I felt it was better to obey the old heads, abide with them, and cooperate with their ideas.

Another point I showed them was this: the longer we stay in the bush fighting, traveling about in the jungle with all kinds of dangerous animals, the more we become like wild, savage people. We are punishing ourselves by living this way.

It was true that many Miskito comandantes had behaved like savages toward their own race. I can think of many Indians who were captured and killed by commanders and fighters. Some were taken on the pretext that they were Sandinista collaborators; others were assassinated for pure pleasure. These Miskitos were killed not by the Sandinistas but by their own Indian brothers. This behavior was like that of animals. Miskitos killing Miskitos is unacceptable in my way of thinking. I was in the mountains many years living like an animal, but that kind of thing I never did. If I captured a Sandinista, I sent him to Honduras to be put in jail. Always I would try to explain to my captives why we Miskito were fighting to reclaim our rights.

At Seven Benk I had captured a Sandinista fighter woman named Maura. She said, "Kill me! I am Sandinista!" I had carried her to my base and offered her food. She said, "I don't want your poisoned food. Kill me! I only want to be dead!" For four days she would not eat or bathe. Always I was talking kindly to her, trying to show her my cause was just, as were my ways. I told her that we were fighting because the government had moved our people out of their homes and had marched them off to faraway camps, then had burned the little villages and slaughtered the chickens, cows, and pigs. I said to the Sandinista woman, "Someday we will have peace. You are not my enemy. You are my sister. We are Nicaraguans." After two weeks had passed the woman told me, "I was wrong. I have made mistakes. Now I know what your rights are and I understand your loss. Ráfaga, if you believe me, give me a gun and I will fight with you." I gave to her a gun and she fought with us against the Sandinistas.

Fagoth and Diego never taught the boys any "rules of war." They just left the methodology to the commanders, and many used savage methods. My education in theology had made me another kind of man. Each time I would leave my base on a mission or start into battle, I would preach to my boys the 121st Psalm. You see, I love this life, the people and the animals. All of us have a right to know the beauty of this world.

We had been fighting that guerrilla war for five years without getting one inch ahead. We had won nothing. In that five years, thousands of Miskito people had died, and hundreds were maimed, crippled, or had their eyes blown out. When I analyzed all this, I saw no hope, only prolonged foolishness and misery. The government jails were full of broken spirits of once proud Indians. Those boys, after they were put in jail, were not whole men. They were like a half or a quarter of a man. Many of them died in jail because their spirits had broken.

Not only the government was to blame for all the atrocities. Miskitos had murdered Miskitos, spilling the blood of our own race. Lies had been told by Miskitos against our own people. Miskito fighters had beaten, raped, and killed their Indian brothers and sisters. If you look at both sides, neither is without fault. Most of the crimes committed against Miskitos by Miskitos were done by lower-ranking fighters making decisions on their own without direct order. But other grossly wicked deeds were done at a comandante's direct order. One example is the kidnapping and rape of a Miskito medical doctor. A wicked commander ordered the kidnapping of the doctor and then permitted sixty-four of his Indian fighters to rape her successively. For a crime such as that, there is no redemption.

I discussed all these points with the comandantes who came from Honduras to destroy us and Yulo. I tried to help them understand that neither side was helping our people. Both sides were giving misery to the Indian civilians in the middle, causing them to suffer more. Many families had run from their river homes to Puerto Cabezas, Bluefields, and Managua. The few who had the means left for the United States, while poorer ones ran to Honduras and to Costa Rica. Sooner or later, if this war continued, there would be no Indians living on the Atlantic Coast of Nicaragua. They would all have disappeared. They all have had to run away because they are afraid of the Sandinistas and they are afraid of the guerrilla Indian fighters.

Another thing I told this group from KISAN por la Guerra was this: this new generation of young Indian is different than ourselves. They have new kinds of ideas about how to make their future better. They are going to Sandinista schools, learning the way of Sandinista law, and being trained to think like Sandinistas. That is why our way of thinking must change, if we are to survive as an Indian nation. It is better that we look for peace. Mauricio Isaias and David Clark returned to Honduras with their fighters.

In August 1986 Diego sent Manuel Cunningham (Tiger no. 17), with eighty fighters, to Yulo. I believe Diego must have been frustrated because all of those comandantes he was sending to finish us and Yulo were returning from failed missions. I believe that is why he sent Tiger no. 17. That bad fellow was a ruthless fighter, and Diego probably thought that this was the right man to kill Ráfaga.

As Tiger no. 17 was coming toward Yulo, not one moment did we ever plan to fight against him. We kept our faith in our hopes for the peace. Just as I had done with Diego's comandantes before, I did with Tiger no. 17. He had come to Yulo intending to fight against us, but the Yulo community met him with a stronger intention: to maintain the peace.

Eventually, all of those KISAN por la Guerra comandantes

and their fighters returned to join with us in the dialogue. Our numbers in Yulo grew so large that we and the government established other peace zones like Yulo, and the peace grew in number and area.

That is how we passed through 1986. We passed by many dangers trying to make a better life. The proof of our efforts is this: We started the dialogue in 1985. Now, in 1987, we are still in dialogue with the government. We love peace. We are proud of our helping to write into the Nicaraguan Constitution a law of autonomy for the Atlantic Coast. Now we must try to make autonomy real, not just be satisfied with words on paper. For us, autonomy will be our victory.

Ráfaga Bara Klaunalaka
By Astin Reyes (Chino)
Miskut, Honduras, 1985
(In Miskito)

Komandante Ráfaga yauhka titan
Like yu raya kum kabia
Pirikuako avion ka sukra naniba
Kli yawan mapara wanmina prukan ka
Kum kabia apia, siran sin wan ikbia apia.
Yawan pri ka bia, klaunalaka ba yawan dukia sa.
Yawan pri ka bia, klaunalaka ba yawan dukia sa.

Wan gol ka ba yawan dukia sa
Wan Yulo ka ba yawan dukia sa
Wan awaska nani ba yawan dukia sa
Wan kabo ka ba yawan dukia sa
Wan tasbaya aiska ba yawan dukia sa.

Wan Almuk nani Awastara
Upli ka nani sut lamtuwan palisa
Komandante praut kira nani
Kaskabel waitni ka, Eduwin Klebland,
Bruno Gabriel, Joaquín Barquero,
Timson Mateo, kumna lupia wan muihni wala
Nani pruwan ba sut asla takan geven ra
Bara Dawan ra makaban klauna laka dukia ra.
Pirikuako nani klaunalaka ba rait daukras sa kaka,

Witin nani geven ba kriki
Kli tasba ra bal aikla bi wapni ka daukisi waya win.
Kosta Atlantica pri apia kaka pruwaya!

Ráfaga and Autonomy

Comandante Ráfaga
Tomorrow will be a new dawning
The Piricuaca (Sandinista) air force
Will no longer be a temptation or a threat.
We will be free, autonomy is ours;
We will be free, autonomy is ours.

Our gold is ours
Our palm oil is ours
Our fishing is ours
Our forests are ours.

The old wise men and women
Of Awastara will venerate you.
The fallen heroes and martyrs—
Comandantes Cascabel, Eduwin Klebland,
Bruno Gabriel, Joaquín Barquero,
Timson Mateo, Cumita, and other fallen brothers—
Form the celestial court where they ask the Lord
For true autonomy.
They ask the Lord
That, if the Piricuacos do not satisfy the desire
Of the spirit of our ancestors,
He should break heaven open and let them come back
To continue the struggle
Until Autonomy is won.
A free Atlantic Coast or death!

Eleven / Matwalsipurakumi

Autonomy

The autonomy of the Atlantic Coast of Nicaragua is not just a recent issue that we Miskitos have asked the Sandinista government to address. We have already been practicing political autonomy for many centuries. The proof of this is a list of our kings: Old Man I (1670); James II (1685–87), crowned in Jamaica; Jeremias (1687); Federico Alexander (1694); Jeremias II (1699); Briton or Carlos Antonio (1787), a Miskito chief assassinated by his nephew Alparis in Tuapi; Edward (1740); George (1791–94), died in 1794 in an uprising; Stephen (1797); George Frederick (1816), assassinated in 1824; Roberto Charles Frederick (1825–41); Jorge Guillermo (1841–45); Jorge Augusto Federick (1845–65); William Henry Klarans (1866–79); Jorge William Klarans (1879–88); Jorge William Albert Henry (1888–90); and Henry Klarans (1891–94), the last king. People can check this with the history books if they want.

Despite our history of autonomy, we have been robbed of our dignity in many ways. A most important way in which this has been done is by disregarding our own names for ourselves and our land. We call the Atlantic Coast of Nicaragua, where our people live, Tawaswalpa. We call ourselves Miskuyo, never Miskito, Mosquito, or Mosco, which all refer to insects, flies. Most Miskuyo who live far from the cities do not even know that others call them Miskitos. We believe that it is an act of cruelty on the part of the mestizos of the Pacific Coast and their governments to have insisted on calling us Miskitos. Their anti-Indianism is so intense that they have called our highest authorities *reyes moscos,* "fly kings." This is due to jealousy and political hatred, mixed with the colonizers' ignorance. Indians, blacks, and other North American minorities will understand this easily because they have experienced the same hateful lack of respect.

Since July 19, 1979, with the disappearance of the dictator Somoza, many discriminatory words also disappeared as if by magic (along with the discriminators, the exploitative landholders). Words like *boss, servant, sir, madam,* and such have been replaced by the terms *compañero* and *compañera.* The Sandinista government has truly liberated us from these national offenses, which were established by capitalist oligarchies and exhibitionist individuals like the Liberal president Jose Santos Zelaya and General Rigoberto Cabezas.

The government of Zelaya took Bluefields militarily on February 12, 1894. More than a hundred Tawaswalpans were killed, dozens wounded, and hundreds were imprisoned. Immediately, Miskuyo authorities were deposed, and in subsequent acts, Tawaswalpa was renamed after Zelaya and our beloved city of Bilwi (Snake Leaves) was declared Puerto Cabezas. What a contrast. What a joke.

These actions were explained to the world as the reincorporation of the Miskito Coast and were immediately supported by the government of the United States, since it thereby gained unique control of the possible canal route.

I have faith and hope that in the near future Tawaswalpa will again be Tawaswalpa. Since only a few years remain before the centennial of these horrible deeds, we can hope that the wise refrain "*No hay mal que cien años dure* [No bad thing can last a hundred years]" still holds true. To initiate this change, I will use the correct terms for my people and our land in the rest of this book.

Choosing authorities for Tawaswalpa is a big concern of ours. We want the highest authorities of autonomy to be genuine *costeños* (coastal people) who think and act in the interests of Tawaswalpa. The Sandinista government is ready to nominate fanatic Miskuyo Sandinistas as candidates, and we don't want that. There are a few Miskuyo chiefs in the ministries of the Sandinista government who unfortunately speak Miskuyo but think in Spanish. We don't want this. They are militants of the Frente Sandinista de Liberación Nacional (FSLN) and are partisan. They want to fulfill the will of the party. If they become the leaders of autonomy, they will always seek to satisfy the interests of the central government. Eminently, we want the highest authority to be a *costeño* who speaks and thinks in terms of the interests of the people on the coast.

Regarding the means for choosing leaders, I disagree with Tomás Borge on a certain point. He speaks of dividing Tawaswalpa into sections and choosing leaders from various parts, like Northern Zelaya, Southern Zelaya, and Central Zelaya. If that is done, these divisions will have problems among each other within ten or twenty years. They may become separatist and seek their rights individually. The people of Bluefields, for instance, might have to pay tariffs to fish in Northern Zelaya. That is a possibility. The autonomy law that has been agreed to by Zelaya and the central government, drawn up mostly by Miskuyo Creole Sandinistas, says that all *costeños* will have the rights to the woods, rivers, seas, and what is underground, but only in the section where they live. For the Miskuyo, Tawaswalpa does not have such sections. Instead we have thirty-eight provinces, each of which will choose its representatives; these assembled representatives will choose the "governor" and his or her cabinet. We may also want the governor to be elected in a democratic election.

For us autonomy does not mean total independence from the constitutional government of Nicaragua. We plan to administer our natural resources on our own—for example, our fish, lumber, minerals, gold, silver, lead, zinc, and so forth—with the approval of the central government if it is necessary. That is, the central government could find us bank loans to begin the exploitation of these resources. They could also help find the international markets. We prefer to market to the Caribbean. We would give a percentage to the government, perhaps 20–30 percent of the profits, with 70–80 percent to remain in the region for us to build clinics, schools, bridges, highways, and churches (the last is important to me as a clergyman), to bring well-being to the people in general.

Since we don't have any resources right now, agriculture is hard to reestablish. We need to reactivate it. Tawaswalpa is a large territory, three times the size of El Salvador, and it is very rich in natural resources despite its exploitation by companies like the Neptune Gold Mining Company.

We also must devote a great deal of attention to social and cultural development. We are lovers of education, but we have a lot of young people who graduate from high school and do not continue in education for lack of resources. We want to prepare them, to send them to study in universities in other countries, and establish a university in Bluefields or Bilwi. This is possible immediately.

For me, autonomy is not a gift from the Sandinistas. The autonomy of Tawaswalpa is a historical right that the Sandinista government has recognized. It has been a fact since May 2, 1987, when it was approved and established in the constitution of Nicaragua as the law. This was a great step for us.

We took up arms originally to claim our historical rights, and we soon found ourselves in a genocidal war between the brothers of Nicaragua, and between the people of Tawaswalpa and the government of Nicaragua. Later the government recognized its errors and mistakes and offered to negotiate with the Indians and recognize the historical rights of Tawaswalpa. Now we need to fight for autonomy at the table with pens in hand, not arms.

As an Indian who loves peace and development and autonomy, I do not want the Sandinistas to make more mistakes, as they did at the beginning of the revolution, with the inhabitants of Tawaswalpa. We want autonomy to be a real example, to be effective, to be a reality, and not to serve as propaganda for the Sandinistas nationally and internationally. Autonomy should not be just a piece of paper with ink on it that is thrown into the wastebasket when the war is over.

I hope that Indians in other parts take the development of our autonomy as an example. I do not recommend that other indigenous nations claim their rights through armed struggle as we did, but if it is necessary, they should do it. Our example can be copied by other peoples, and the great example of the revolutionary government of Nicaragua should be copied by other governments in Central and South America—and why not in North America, too? Why not cede the historical right to autonomy to the Indians? I put special emphasis on the governments of Guatemala, Honduras, Bolivia, and Brazil.

To make autonomy real in Nicaragua or in any part of the world, many aspects of the arrangements will have to be specified. We will have to see what sorts of international guarantees of autonomy can be established. Financial and economic arrangements will have to be carefully thought through in order to fend off intrusion by other interests. Perhaps some of this will be accomplished through joint work with the international Indian movement. Perhaps wealthy Indians will play a key role in providing the capital we will need. All of these details will need to be considered in the near future. There is obviously much work to do.

Twelve / Matwalsippurawal

Legacy of a Guerrillero/Peacemaker

NOVEMBER 13, 1987

My work has not been for nothing. I have to believe that it has been valuable. Ulu with his group and Mauricio with his fighters are all in the dialogue now. Another comandante, Uriel Vanegas, came back to get into the dialogue just a little more than one month ago. About twenty days ago Comandante Maximo returned to his country with thirty-five men to work in peaceful ways with KISAN por la Paz and the government. This shows me that our work to bring peace between us and the government is bearing fruit. I am thinking that by this time next year, there will be very few Indians left to fight a war from the Honduran and Costa Rican borders. Only Diego and few of his officers continue to ignore the Autonomy Statute and refuse to enter the dialogue with their brothers and sisters.

Today a Managua newspaper, *Barricada,* reports that Wycliffe Diego is planning another attack on Yulo and vows to kill Comandante Ráfaga. Well, I believe that my Indian brother will have to come on his own for that mission because the comandantes who used to do his bidding are here with us working for the peace. There is a seat at the peace table with Wycliffe's name on it. Let him come to see me so that I can convince him to sit in it.

Brooklyn Rivera, Steadman Fagoth, and Wycliffe Diego have all been under the direction of outsiders. I believe that our friends in foreign nations should give us their ideas. That is not a bad thing or a wrong thing. But I do not believe that our

174

Indian leaders in Honduras or Costa Rica or in Miami Beach can know how life really is, now, in our country. They have been away too long and have been taking advice from people, many of whom have never set their feet on Nicaraguan soil. I, Ráfaga, the Comandante Ráfaga, who am here among my people, can see what our problems are—I can feel what the problems do to us, how they change us.

I have wise men and women here with me who can see the situation of our country, like my uncle Abraham and others who live here with an understanding of the problems we have. Those are the kinds of men and women from whom I take counsel. I do not take direction from other parts of the world.

My counselors have not been scientific men, not men of high study, nor anthropologists, nor Washington lawyers; rather, they have been those old heads who have lived since an older time than I, and who have survived all this difficulty we have been passing through from that time into this time. They are the ones in whom I have confidence. They give me real hope.

I believe that Diego, Rivera, and Fagoth must have some kind of promises with the CIA and others that keep them in an opposition. That might be the reason why they will not or cannot return to their own country where they were born and grew up.

It is very important for all to know that our Indian people in Nicaragua do not want to have any participation with the Somocista National Guard. We are separate from that group. Those leaders, like Alfonso Robelo, Enrique Bermudez, Adolfo Calero, and others with them in Miami Beach are fighting a war against the Sandinistas to regain the money and the political power they lost in the revolution. Unlike those people, we the Indians never had big factories or mansions or big plantations. Those Somocistas had all those things in Managua, on the Pacific side. That is why they are fighting now to get it back.

We the Indians do not want anything great or big. We are only demanding our human rights that are due us. For more than forty-five years the Somocistas had us under their feet, keeping us down, and we will never allow that to be the way of our country again.

During Somoza's time, his select few took our national resources from Tawaswalpa or allowed companies from other
nations to exploit them. But they never put anything back.
Never did they help us to build hospitals or schools or roads.
Now, through our Autonomy Statute, we are being helped by
the government to restore those losses, improve our roads,
our schools, and our industries. But the rebellious ones who
continue to make war bring hardship and obstacles to slow
our progress. I believe those leaders in Honduras, Costa Rica,
and Miami Beach like war because they profit from it. By having
this war, they have more money. The war is their business.
When the war is over, where will they have their business?
Where will they make another war?

Not everything in war is bad. When I was fighting in the
jungle, life was hard, but there was a peculiar sweetness about
the way my boys and I survived together. In that respect, the
warring had in it some good qualities.

In the jungle we lived together for days, weeks, and months,
depending on each other for our very lives. We call this *espiritu
de cuerpo* (esprit de corps). We had a profound love for each
other. When I was shot, they would pick me up and carry me.
When they were shot, I carried them in my arms. I would feel
their pain and I would say, "*Hermano y compañero de lucha!*
[Brother and comrade in struggle]." That is *espíritu de cuerpo.*
We were of the same flesh surviving in spite of the forces of
man and because of the gifts of nature. This created in us a
vengeance toward our enemy and a respect for our mother,
Nature. We killed the enemy and learned much from our
mother, the jungle.

In this world many strange things happen. In the world things
happen that are impossible to explain and hard to believe. But
we who have been in the jungle for so long, sometimes lost
without food or water, do know that she, the jungle, will help
us. She gives us a place to sleep, shows us where there is
water, guides and nourishes us if we listen to her. If we are lost,
she guides us to a place of safety and comfort.

We have a large vine in the mountains called *bejuco,* which
hangs from trees. Inside the *bejuco* is crystal clear water. When

we cut the vine, the good water gushes out like water from a garden hose. That is the best water in the whole world. It has a rich taste, and I believe it must contain many good minerals and vitamins.

There in the mountains are roots that my Indian brothers and sisters have to eat. They are as good as food. Also, from the bark of the mangrove and *nancite* we get a juice. That is the best juice that we have for the men. Because we walk so much in the jungle and through the water, we often have a fungus on our feet. The juice drys and kills the fungus. We put the juice inside our boots and in that way we can go for two or three weeks without the fungus bothering our feet.

The jungle makes us knowledgeable and makes us real men with strong souls. There in the jungle we have been closer to God than anyone. We have great faith in God because nature talks and says all of the beautiful things of that higher power. We also feel the powerful hand of God there in the mountains. The power is contained in the beautiful structure of every thing and creature.

When we feel worried or lost, birds and crickets sing to us. In their songs we hear the voice of God. We passed through many months in the mountains without seeing another human. Sometimes we had much sadness because we would lose a brother in the fighting. We would try to comfort each other in those times, but it was nature that nourished our souls so that we would feel again like fighting.

Many times we would go for five or six days without food or the crystal clear water that I spoke of before or the roots. Sometimes we could find neither roots nor vines. There are places in the jungle where there is much and places where there is nothing. It was always nature that guided us to our food and comfort. Many times I would say to the boys, "These birds and animals do not work, neither do they have money or food, and yet they are still alive. So we also shall continue to live. I am not going to die because I do not have food today." That is how I would comfort my boys who were worried and frightened.

The more worried I was, the more clearly nature would show

her secrets to me. The beautiful birds of a thousand colors would start to sing to us. I would interpret the bird songs: "Fighting is hard. All of the birds are telling us that any day, at any moment, the people will stop their fighting." Some of the boys did not believe I could understand the songs of the birds, but others would think deeply inside themselves about the message and its source. Sooner or later they would say, "Yes, my brother Ráfaga, you are a man with a great faith and you are our commander. With you we will go all the way to the end, because you believe in God and because God has a road through the universe that your feet are upon."

One time I was with a group of fifteen boys in a place called Ulan Awala. We had escaped from the Sandinistas and the government had sent soldiers to capture us. There was no road to take, and the soldiers were close behind, so we started running into the jungle. After many hours we came to a river about fifteen yards wide and very deep. There was no other way to continue on except to turn and confront the soldiers who were pursuing us. So we decided to cross the river. We did not have time to think about a plan. We had to act very fast. I counted three large alligators in that place, and the enemy was coming quickly after us. It is not right to kill animals, but I did have to give the order to kill those alligators so the boys and I could swim to the other side of the river safely.

When we had gotten into the river about ten yards from the bank, I saw those animals coming toward us. Our rifles were in our backpacks, and we swam with our knives in our mouths. These animals coming toward me had sensitive expressions as though they were not going to harm us, but I gave the order to kill them. I Ráfaga, killed one and two of my boys killed the others while the rest of our group swam on over to the other side. Our strategy was to dive under the water two yards before we came face-to-face with the alligators, come up underneath them, then stick our knives into their soft bellies. We knew full well that alligators could go underwater also, but we had to try to kill them this way because the soft belly is the only vulnerable place on the animal's body. There in the middle of the water, we stuck them good and ripped those bellies from side to side.

I remember being under the water and holding one of the animal's feet while sticking and ripping it with my knife. That alligator was about fourteen feet long and very hungry. All three were hungry. When I had finished with the killing I swam to the other side, got out, and looked back to see the river running red with blood. We were all lucky, and those of us who had fought with the animals were exhausted. I checked on my boys, all of whom were safe.

I had suspected that the Sandinistas would not go into the river, and they did not. If they had tried to swim across, they would have been eaten, for many more animals were coming then. We took a position and made a little camp on our side of the river where we could see the government soldiers as they took a position on the other side. It was a big group—perhaps fifty or sixty. Seeing that we had made it across, and seeing the dead animals in the water, they were intelligent enough not to try anything so adventurous.

The breeze was blowing from their side to ours, so it was easy to hear the conversations of the soldiers. It was then that we learned the truth of the situation. One of the soldiers said, "Honestly, those Indians should be honored and praised. They are more savage than the alligators. They are truly great men." We also overheard them saying, "Son of a bitch! We've lost their tracks. Now we are more lost than ever!" Those Sandinistas had not been chasing us to capture us. They had been following us so they could find their way out of the jungle. We listened to them discussing this for a long time. It was only a coincidence that those soldiers had become lost in the jungle at just the same time that we were running away from the Sandinistas in Ulan Awala. That was just one of life's sad but funny little stories.

We kept hidden the rest of the afternoon, and when night came down we built a fire so the government soldiers could locate us. Immediately we left our camp, continuing on through the jungle. As we traveled, we marked trees so the soldiers would be able to find their way out of that place and be safe. I never found out exactly what happened to those Sandinistas, but I think they probably found their way out by crossing the river at a safer place. Maybe they made a raft. Then they found our camp and the mark we left on the trees. I believe this must be true because those particular Sandinistas were intelligent and brave, in that they passed through all of the danger that we had.

Animals that you have read about or seen in the movies, we see for real in the jungle. We see many kinds of large jungle cats, including jaguars and ocelots. When these animals find a human, they have an instinct to kill and destroy. There are also large serpents in the jungle, which we call she-snakes. They get to be friendly toward us Indians and often follow us in the road for many miles. Sometimes a she-snake will become so friendly with my Indian brothers that they can play and talk with her and she will walk along beside them for a long time, just like a pet.

Other snakes are very dangerous. My boys many times have been bitten by *cascabel* (rattlesnakes) and also by snakes called yellowbeard. We have several methods of curing ourselves when we have been bitten by poisonous snakes. In some cases, we bite the snake. But one must have good teeth to bite a poisonous snake in this way. Also, we have herbs that cure the bite. Using another method, we burn the snake's head, then rub the ashes into the wound. I do not know if science or modern medicine knows of our methods, but we Miskuyo, Sumo, and Rama Indians have been practicing these ways for many hundreds of years. There is another snake, the boa, which can be twenty feet long. This snake is always ready to destroy you. All of these creatures are in the jungles and mountains of Nicaragua. When I think about my past experiences with these animals, I feel confounded, but that was just a part of my life. The fear, the hunger, and the desperation— that too was a part of my life in the mountains.

Another day, I was lost. I was also hungry and sad. A bird of a thousand colors came to me that day and saved me and my boys, who were feeling worried. The bird, which weighed about fourteen ounces, started to sing right in front of me, and he was jumping and flying from side to side. I said to myself, "Here comes a bird that sings and plays with me." I made myself to understand his language and his song, and I whistled back to him that we were lost and worried. This little bird made many gestures and many expressions toward me, and then he flew away. When my friend of a thousand colors returned to me, I said, "How good is my life. Even the birds like me. Even the birds sing to me. How good is my God." I told the bird, "God is good to me and I will follow you." I told the little bird how happy I was to have him for a friend and that my boys and I would listen to what he had to tell us. I was the oldest of the group and I was the comandante.

From early in the morning we followed the bird as he flew. My little friend of a thousand colors would fly from tree to tree and sometimes he would stop and sing to me. I tried very hard never to lose sight of him, and I would tell the boys what his songs were telling us. We were exhausted, but I told the boys, "We cannot quit now. We are getting closer to the real road or maybe close to a village." The boys kept on following me and I kept on following my little friend. Then I saw the bird becoming more and more impatient. Suddenly the bird flew far away, then returned. Again he flew away and was out of my sight for a long time. But I could hear him calling me, and I followed his song until we came upon a place where there were four little houses. The houses were empty. All around were many fruit-laden trees. We ate oranges and coconuts, then found the road, which took us to safety. That is exactly how it happened to us in the midst of our worries that the little friend of a thousand colors rescued us from the jungle. That bird is like an Indian fighter. He belongs to the Indians. He saved our lives, so I named that bird *aiklaklabra knawira* (the bird of the Indian fighter).

In the jungle we feed ourselves with leaves that look like orange tree leaves, maybe a little smaller. They make a delicious tea. The leaf contains milk and sugar, and it smells like an orange. There are some places where we find this leaf and in others it does not grow at all. The day that the white man discovers this leaf, its riches will be exploited, because it is full of vitamins and very rich.

Nature and her gifts have made us knowledgeable guerrillas. There are places in the jungle where we can fish and feed about ten men. There are other places near the rivers and ocean where we can find food enough for not just ten but for one hundred or more men. When we are in those places we make harpoons and hooks out of sticks to catch the fish.

In the jungle are big trees that we call ceiba, Santa Maria, and *coa.* These trees contain much mystery and knowledge, which they give to guerrillas who understand them. These trees are all very special to us, especially the ceiba. The roots of the ceiba are large, and branch out from the trunk high above the ground to create roomlike spaces beneath them. Men can actually live in those spaces. When older guerrillas, like myself, Laihn Pihni, Laihn Pauni, Cascavel, Sutum, Tunki, and others go into those spaces between the roots of the ceiba, we receive the knowledge of the tree. When I concentrate at the base of the tree, the tree indicates from which direction the enemy is coming and gives me other ideas and strange sounds. It is not easy to perceive these things. We who know the way must concentrate and listen very hard in just the right place. We Miskuyo have been getting such understanding and knowledge from the mountains of Tawaswalpa for hundreds of years.

I would like for these things to be published someday in the Miskuyo language so my Indian brothers and sisters and our Indian children may read and understand this history in our native language. They would enjoy reading this book because many of these things have happened during their own lives. Indian men like Tunki, Sutum, Guillermo Recta, Juan Salgado, Barbon, Cebre, Waiti, and Mauricio Isaias—all of whom are good fighters and good leaders—may someday read this history and know that our struggle was not in vain. In a future time, perhaps ten or fifty or a hundred years from now, this recorded history may help an Indian child, a community, or even a nation to understand and remember the trouble through which we all passed because we wanted our people and our heritage to survive.

Epilogue

You can be the judge of my feelings and of what I have reported here. I have told you only what I saw and heard and how it made me feel and think. I will not judge this history.

Now, I am not against any man or government past or present. As you have read my story, you no doubt have noticed that I spoke sometimes in favor of a government, then against it. This is intended not to confuse you but rather to enlighten you to the complexity of our life on Nicaragua's Atlantic Coast.

My only desire is that you might know from my perspective this history of Tawaswalpa, my homeland. My history is the only history to which I can testify.

I know there are other written versions of life in Nicaragua from other perspectives because I have read some of them, and I encourage you to read them also. I like to have all of the evidence before I make a judgment or form an opinion, just as you do.

The heroes and martyrs who gave their lives in this Indian revolution sacrificed themselves so that the Miskuyo nation could reclaim its rights and protect its sacred principles. There is a distinct division between the two groups of people fighting against our government, and my testimony is for the Indian faction of that fight, not for the Somocista National Guard faction, often referred to as the Contras.

Many of the Indian fighters who died in my arms were fathers who with their last breath begged me to help their sons and daughters if God spared my life. This responsibility I have accepted.

Since May 1988 I have been in the United States speaking to university and church groups, trying my best to inform the people of the United States about our situation. I have also tried to gather money and material aid for the more than four thousand war orphans. Even though many of those to whom I have spoken sympathize with the needs of the orphans, they are reluctant to give much because they cannot be assured that a totally stable organization is in place in Tawaswalpa to administer funds and develop projects. The fact remains that the orphans continue to suffer.

It is my hope that the royalties from this book will be a new beginning toward meeting the needs of those Indian children. A portion of the royalties will be used to supply immediate needs such as food and medicine, but the greater portion will be placed in a scholarship fund to be used for the children's higher education.

The success or failure of autonomy depends on whether we Miskuyo can successfully administer our law and our economy. In order to do this, we must become educated. It is true that there exists much political instability, but I have tried to realize this goal in spite of the many difficulties.

The recent election, in February 1990, of Doña Violeta Barrios de Chamorro and the National Opposition Union (UNO), displacing the "comrades" in Nicaragua, is definitely the triumph of liberty, peace, justice, development, and national reconciliation. July 19, 1979, was for me and for many Nicaraguans a joyous day. The church bells rang as people banged any piece of metal they could find in celebration. But the victory of Doña Violeta and Dr. Godoy Reyes is without equal in our history. There will be no summary executions of the losers, nor political exiles. Ministers will be free to preach the gospel as it should be preached. If there are confiscations, they will not be capricious ones. With Doña Violeta, justice and freedom of expression will reign. For the first time since its independence from Spain in 1821, Nicaragua will not be run by boss-fathers who have made Nicaragua into their personal ranches. Now we will have a mother who will know how to guide the desires and hopes of each of her wild sons. Our mother will fulfill the desires of our heroes and martyrs, accomplishing the dream of our immortal poet Rubén Darío, who would say: *Si la patria es pequeña, UNO grande la sueña.* The struggle of our martyr Pedro Joaquín Chamorro is finally realized: *¡Nicaragua volverá ser República!* The desires and dreams of the indigenous nation will be realized as well. Tawaswalpa will again be Tawaswalpa. With Doña Violeta, our autonomy will be real and effective, not just a piece of paper.

Doña Violeta's task will not be easy, but if she helps peace, liberty, and freedom to grow, she will be able to count on the support of her people. They simply want to enjoy their family life with a roof over their heads, with jobs and bread. While the experts tried in vain to predict the outcome of the election, the hearts of the *campesinos* knew what they desired. True heroes want only freedom for their families to grow in peace. They are the ones who say, "Here I am. Tell me what to do, and I'll do it."

Right now the Miskuyos are working hard to maintain a stable peace with dignity. Their struggle is not reported in any newspaper, book, or television program. Still, my brothers and sisters keep on with the struggle because we want to survive as a nation.

My hope is that someday in the future a way will be found to publish this book in the Miskuyo language. Then the Indians will know that the people of the world have been notified and therefore have the opportunity to add their hopes and their energies to our struggle.

Many of us, since 1985, have worked hard to bring peace without bloodshed to our homeland. We have not been given any prize, nor have we been recognized by any country, government, or organization for this work, but we have received appreciation from our Indian people. For me, this has been the greatest gift.

In the midst of my worst troubles in the jungle, when I was suffering, wounded, bleeding, and full of infection, I knew the presence of an energy inside myself that was full of happiness and hopefulness that someday Nicaragua and the world would understand why we make these sacrifices. We want to live in dignity and health. That day is dawning now. You have this history in your hands.

My mother's advice has always been beautiful for me. When I first told her about the plans Judy Wilson and I had to write this history, she advised me to try hard to remember everything correctly as I had experienced and felt it because my mother knows that there is much energy born out of truth. By the time you have read this history, the life of my mother will probably have passed, for she suffers now with terminal cancer.

I want to thank my friends in the United States and in Nicaragua for their support and advice regarding my participation in this project. Especially, I feel grateful to our old heads, who advised me to follow this project to completion because they, like my mother, believe that the world must know this history.

Further Reading

The journal *Nicaribe: Revista de la costa atlantica*. Published in Bluefields, Nicaragua.

The journal *Nicaraguan Perspectives*. Published by the Nicaragua Information Center, Berkeley, California.

Americas Watch. 1984. *The Miskitos in Nicaragua, 1981–1984*. New York: Americas Watch Committee.

Bell, Charles N. 1899. *Tangweera: Life and adventures among gentle savages*. London: E. Arnold.

CIDCA–Development Study Unit Staff, ed. 1987. *Ethnic groups and the nation state: The case of the Atlantic Coast in Nicaragua*. Stockholm: Stockholms Universitet/Coronet Books.

Conzemius, E. 1932. *Ethnographical survey of the Miskito and Sumu Indians*. Smithsonian Institution, Bureau of American Ethnology, Bulletin no. 106. Washington, D.C.: U.S. Government Printing Office.

Dodds, D. 1989. Miskito and Sumu refugees: Caught in conflict in Honduras. *Cultural Survival Quarterly 13*(3): 3–6.

Dunbar Ortiz, R. 1988. *The Miskito indians of Nicaragua*. Minority Rights Group Report no. 79. London: Minority Rights Group.

Macdonald, T., Jr. 1984a. Miskito refugees in Costa Rica. *Cultural Survival Quarterly 8*(3): 59–60.

———. 1984b. Misurasata goes home. *Cultural Survival Quarterly 8*(4): 42–49.

———. 1985. Advances toward a Miskito-Sandinista cease-fire. *Cultural Survival Quarterly 9*(2), 38–42.

Newson, L. A. 1987. *Indian survival in colonial Nicaragua*. Norman: University of Oklahoma Press.

Nietschmann, B. 1973. *Between land and water: the subsistence ecology of the Miskito Indians.* New York: Seminar Press.

————. 1987. The Third World war. *Cultural Survival Quarterly* *11*(3): 1–16.

————. 1989. *The unknown war: The Miskito nation, Nicaragua, and the United States.* Focus on Issues, no. 8. Freedom House/University Press of America.

Rosengarten, Frederic, 1976. *Freebooters must die!: The life and death of William Walker, the most notorious filibuster of the nineteenth century.* Wayne, Pa.: Haverford House.

Smith, C. A., J. Boyer, and M. Diskin. 1988. Central America since 1979, part 2. *Annual Review of Anthropology* 17:331–64.

Tazewell, J., ed. *The Miskito question and the revolution in Nicaragua.* Hampton, Va.: Compita Publishing, Tidewater Nicaragua Project Foundation.

Wright, R. M. 1988. Anthropological presuppositions of indigenous advocacy. *Annual Review of Anthropology* 17:365–90.

Index